M000220426

Prepare for the Great Tribulation and the Era of Peace

Prepare for the Great Tribulation and the Era of Peace

Volume VIII:
July 1, 1997 – September 30, 1997

by John Leary

Queenship

PUBLISHING COMPANY
P.O Box 42028 Santa Barbara, CA 93140-2028
(800) 647-9882 • (805) 957-4893 • Fax: (805) 957-1631

The publisher recognizes and accepts that the final authority regarding these apparitions and messages rests with the Holy See of Rome, to whose judgement we willingly submit.

– The Publisher

Cover art by Josyp Terelya

©1997 Queenship Publishing

Library of Congress Number # 97-68596

Published by:
    Queenship Publishing
    P.O. Box 42028
    Santa Barbara, CA 93140-2028
    (800) 647-9882 • (805) 957-4893 • Fax: (805) 957-1631

Printed in the United States of America

ISBN: 1-57918-053-1

Acknowledgments

It is in a spirit of deep gratitude that I would like to acknowledge first the Holy Trinity: Father, Jesus, and the Holy Spirit, the Blessed Virgin Mary and the many saints and angels who have made this book possible.

My wife, Carol, has been an invaluable partner. Her complete support of faith and prayers has allowed us to work as a team. This was especially true in the many hours of indexing and proofing of the manuscript. All of our family has been a source of care and support.

I am greatly indebted to Josyp Terelya for his very gracious offer to provide the art work for this publication. He has spent three months of work and prayer to provide us with a selection of many original pictures. He wanted very much to enhance the visions and messages with these beautiful and provocative works. You will experience some of them throughout these volumes.

A very special thank you goes to my spiritual director, Fr. Leo J. Klem, C.S.B. No matter what hour I called him, he was always there with his confident wisdom, guidance and discernment. His love, humility, deep faith and trust are a true inspiration.

My appreciation also goes to Father John V. Rosse, my good pastor at Holy Name of Jesus Church. He has been open, loving and supportive from the very beginning.

There are many friends and relatives whose interest, love and prayerful support have been a real gift from God. Our own Wednesday, Monday and First Saturday prayer groups deserve a special thank you for their loyalty and faithfulness.

Finally, I would like to thank Bob and Claire Schaefer of Queenship Publishing for providing the opportunity to bring this message of preparation, love and warnings to you the people of God.

John Leary, Jr.

Dedication

To the Most Holy Trinity

God

The Father, Son and Holy Spirit

The Source of

All

Life, Love and Wisdom

Publisher's Foreword

John has, with some exceptions, been having visions twice a day since they began in July, 1993. The first vision of the day usually takes place during morning Mass, immediately after he receives the Eucharist. If the name of the church is not mentioned, it is a local Rochester, NY, church. When out of town, the church name is included in the text. The second vision occurs in the evening, either at Perpetual Adoration or at the prayer group that is held at Holy Name of Jesus Church.

Various names appear in the text. Most of the time, the names appear only once or twice. Their identity is not important to the message and their reason for being in the text is evident. First names have been used, when requested by the individual. The name Maria E., which occurs quite often, is the visionary Maria Esperanza Bianchini of Betania, Venezuela.

We are grateful to Josep Terelya for the cover art, as well as for the art throughout the book. Josyp is a well-known visionary and also, the author of *Witness* and most recently *In the Kingdom of the Spirit.*

This volume covers visions from July 1, 1997 through September 30, 1997. The volumes will now be coming out quarterly due to the urgency of the messages. Volume I contains messages from July, 1993 through June, 1994. Volume II contains messages from July, 1994 through June, 1995. Volume III contains messages from July, 1995 through July 10, 1996. Volume IV contains messages from July 11, 1996 through September 30, 1996. Volume V contains messages from October 1, 1996 through December 31, 1996. Volume VI contains messages from January 1, 1997 through March 31, 1997. Volume VII contains messages from April 1, 1997 through June 30, 1997.

The Publisher

Foreword

It was in July of 1993 that Almighty God, especially through Jesus, His Eternal Word, entered the life of John Leary in a most remarkable way. John is 54 years old and works as a chemist at Eastman Kodak Co., Rochester, New York. He lives in a modest house in the suburbs of Rochester with Carol, his wife of thirty-one years, and Catherine, his youngest daughter. His other two daughters, Jeanette and Donna, are married and have homes of their own. John has been going to daily Mass since he was seventeen and has been conducting a weekly prayer group in his own home for twenty-five years. For a long time, he has been saying fifteen decades of the Rosary each day.

In April of 1993 he and his wife made a pilgrimage to Our Lady's shrine in Medjugorje, Yugoslavia. While there, he felt a special attraction to Jesus in the Blessed Sacrament. There he became aware that the Lord Jesus was asking him to change his way of life and to make Him his first priority. A month later in his home, Our Lord spoke to him and asked if he would give over his will to Him to bring about a very special mission. Without knowing clearly to what he was consenting, John, strong in faith and trust, agreed to all the Lord would ask.

On July 21, 1993 the Lord gave him an inkling of what would be involved in this new calling. He was returning home from Toronto in Canada where he had listened to a talk of Maria Esperanza (a visionary from Betania, Venezuela) and had visited Josyp Terelya. While in bed, he had a mysterious interior vision of a newspaper headline that spelled "DISASTER." Thus began a series of daily and often twice daily interior visions along with messages, mostly from Jesus. Other messages were from God the Father, the Holy Spirit, the Blessed Virgin Mary, his guardian angel and many of the saints, especially St. Therese of Lisieux. These messages he recorded on his word processor. In the beginning, they were quite short, but they became more extensive as the weeks passed by. At the time of this writing, he is still receiving visions and messages.

These daily spiritual experiences, which occur most often immediately following Communion, consist of a brief vision which becomes the basis of the message that follows. They range widely on a great variety of subjects, but one might group them under the following categories: warnings, teachings and love messages. Occasionally, there are personal confirmations of some special requests that he made to the Lord.

The interior visions contain an amazing number of different pictures, some quite startling, which hardly repeat themselves. In regard to the explicit messages that are inspired by each vision, they contain deep insights into the kind of relationship God wishes to establish with His human creatures. There, also, is an awareness of how much He loves us and yearns for our response. As a great saint once wrote: "Love is repaid only by love." On the other hand, God is not a fool to be treated lightly. In fact, did not Jesus once say something about not casting pearls before the swine? Thus, there are certain warnings addressed to those who shrug God off as if He did not exist or is not important in human life.

Along with such warnings, we become more conscious of the reality of Satan and the forces of evil "...which wander through the world seeking the ruin of souls." We used to recite this at the end of each low Mass. In His love and concern for us, Our Lord keeps constantly pointing out how frail we humans are in the face of such evil angelic powers. God is speaking of the necessity of daily prayer, of personal penance, and of turning away from atheistic and material enticements which are so much a part of our modern environment.

Perhaps the most controversial parts of the messages are those which deal with what we commonly call Apocalyptic. Unusual as these may be, in my judgment, they are not basically any different than what we find in the last book of the New Testament or in some of the writings of St. Paul. After a careful and prayerful reading of the hundreds of pages in this book, I have not found anything contrary to the authentic teaching authority of the Roman Catholic Church.

The 16th Century Spanish mystic, St. John of the Cross, gives us sound guidelines for discerning the authenticity of this sort of phenomena involving visions, locutions, etc. According to him, there are three possible sources: the devil, some kind of self-imposed hypnosis or God. I have been John's spiritual confidant for over three years. I have tested him in various spiritual ways and I am most confident that all he has put into these messages is neither of the devil nor of some kind of mental illness. Rather, they are from the God who, in His love for us, wishes to reveal His own Divine mind and heart. He has used John for this. I know that John is quite ready to abide by any decision of proper ecclesiastical authority on what he has written in this book.

Rev. Leo J. Klem, C.S.B.
Rochester, New York

Visions and Messages of John Leary:

Tuesday, July 1, 1997:

After Communion, I could see a pyramid shaped instrument that had a clock face on it. Jesus said, *"My people, time is running out on all of those people with pride and position that have lorded it over the rest. These evil people in authority have caused many wars and have abused other men to gain their wealth and power. These same men have persecuted Me by causing pain to those Christians following Me. Their fate is inevitable and My hand will fall against them in the end. Much like Sodom and Gomorrah were punished by fire from Heaven, these monied men will face My blazing wrath in a short time. My faithful, you cannot have two masters. You cannot be My disciples and love money and all of the things of this world. You must come to Me as little children in obedience to My Will. Seek My love which awaits all of you when you will come into My Kingdom."*

Later, at Adoration, I could look out of a doorway to see some homeless people. Jesus said, *"My people, do not be taken back if you are asked to suffer for My Name's sake. Once you step outside away from your comfort zone, there will be many more trials. Those, who speak in My Name to save souls and seek conversion, will see the price of saving souls requires a commitment to take on more suffering for those souls. When you teach My love to those who hate Me, you are always taking a risk. Unless the missionaries took on this risk, My Word would not have reached many souls. So, it is important to evangelize souls at any opportunity without concern for the consequences of those who may criticize you. I have given My messengers a hard task in delivering My Word to those souls who would be lost otherwise. See that once you have understood My Word, you need to share My love with others. You are responsible to go out and bring My Word to all who will listen. Many are searching for God and need someone to offer my invitation. I ask each of you to carry out the mission I have given you. Do it with joy and do not worry about any persecution."*

Wednesday, July 2, 1997:

After Communion, I could see a segment of rock with an outline indicating it to be the cornerstone. Jesus said, *"My people, in the readings you are seeing how important people treat their birthright. The promise made for many nations coming from Isaac brought about a rejection of Ishmael. I adopted Israel as My people, but when I came to redeem them, My Messiahship was not what they wanted. I, too, was rejected, but still I became the cornerstone of My Church and My Popes are now the successors of My Church. You should see that when God directs something to be, it will succeed against all attempts to destroy it. I have left you with My promise that the gates of Hell will never prevail over My Church. There have been splits and turmoil in My Church, but still the Remnant survives. There will still be another split during the Tribulation, but I will still protect My Remnant against all attempts by Satan to destroy it. My power reigns over the just and the unjust, but My Church will always survive all attempts to destroy it."*

Later, at Adoration, I could see an amusement park and a circling ride which looked like the sign of the warning I have seen before. Jesus said, *"My son, many keep asking you the time of the warning, but I only have given you before what I will tell you. Again, I warn My faithful not to worry about the dates of the coming events. I have heard your question if the warning will occur before the time of the Antichrist's declaration. Many will need a supernatural sign to warn them against taking the mark of the beast before the Antichrist declares himself the christ and ruler of the Earth. I will give you a sign of the truth of this statement at an appropriate time. When this sign is given, you will know when to proclaim the depth of this message. At this time, wait for when this information will be needed. Do not fear, My people, I will guide all those who trust in Me. The Antichrist will reign a short time, but I will protect those souls who seek My help."*

Thursday, July 3, 1997: (St. Thomas, the Apostle)

After Communion, I could see a young face of Jesus radiant in His glorified Body. Jesus said, *"My people, blessed are My faithful who have believed in Me without actually seeing Me in person. If you truly believe, then you are seeing Me in My Real Presence in the Consecrated Host. Give honor and glory to your God for all the many blessings being poured over you. You have been blessed with a strong gift of faith, a gift of life on this Earth, and a gift of My infinite love which gives you peace in all you do. At every Communion you should give thanks to Me for all I have done for each of you. You should be joyous that I have redeemed you from your sins. I have opened the gates of Heaven to each soul seeking forgiveness and desiring to be with My ever loving heart. Rejoice in My love and peace which is being poured out abundantly on all of you."*

Later, at the prayer group, I could see a long large white vinyl pipe for sewers. Jesus said, *"My people, be attentive to the destruction going on around you. You think that you are in control of things until a tornado comes by and you lose your power. Man is in a delicate balance with the powers in the world about you. When you are humbled by these events, it is good so your pride does not puff you up. When you see how futile your efforts of grandeur are, come to Me in submitting your will to follow Me. My love awaits your understanding of seeking Me for your eternal salvation. Once you see My light through the eyes of faith, you will wonder how you could refuse Me."*

I could see some bomber airplanes and they were destroying some ships in flames. Jesus said, *"My people, you will see more wars and efforts by certain nations to acquire land from others. Until you accept My peace among you, you will continue to see the destruction of war in your evil age. The greed and power seeking of your current leaders will cause continuous problems that could involve many nations."*

I could see the U.S. flag and some earlier wars for freedom. Jesus said, *"My people, as you celebrate your Independence Day, think of all the lives that were sacrificed for your physical freedoms. Your forefathers have fought to win this right to rule yourselves. This can be contrasted to the spiritual freedom I have won for you by My suffering on the Cross. Your physical freedom may be contested, but your opportunity to come to Heaven will always be ready for you to embrace."*

I could see Mary coming as she outstretched her mantle of protection. Mary said, *"My dear son, be willing to open your doors to all those who wish to visit you. Welcome them with a special*

*love of my Son, Jesus, so you can share the love of our Two Hearts
with all who come. It is the love and peace of these messages that
will attract many who are seeking this love of God. Share your
time with all of those seeking to better their souls through a conversion in their lives."*

I could see some children reaching out for food to be given
them. Jesus said, *"My people, I have asked you in previous messages to prepare for this evil age by storing up what little food
you can. I have shown you how your weather will threaten your
food supplies. Now, you are coming to understand even more how
Satan's one world people are contriving means to control people
through your food. If you follow My instructions to store food,
your needs will be provided for."*

I could see a set of stairs and a light shining in from a window
at the head of the stairs. Jesus said, *"My people, I am showing
these stairs as a pathway to Me. If you wish to come to Me, you
must advance in your spirituality through My help. Seek to do
better each day, so you can advance along this stairway to Heaven.
If you are to arrive at your destination, you must struggle to give
your will over to Me. It is carrying your daily cross for Me that
will gain you your prize. Never look back, but move forward with
your gaze ever fixed on Me."*

I could see a tabernacle placed in between a husband and wife.
Jesus said, *"My dear spouses, you must come in marriage with
Me as your partner in faith. I give you the grace of this sacrament to keep unity in your family and the blessings of new life.
Love your spouses as the example I give you in My love for My
Church. I have joined you together in My service. See that you
are faithful to one another as I ask your faithfulness in loving
Me. There will be great joy to see your family weather the trials
of life and still remain united in love. Many rejoice to see married couples who have advanced in older age together. Give thanks
to God for these lasting marriages."*

Friday, July 4, 1997: (Independence Day)

After Communion, I could see a priest at the altar with the older
vestments on. Jesus said, *"My dear people, I am calling on My
faithful remnant to preserve My Church in the face of this evil*

age. Many have been drawn to save books, vestments, and vessels. You may need them soon when another split will come into My Church. Modernism has attacked the roots of My Church and many want to be up to date with the latest changes. It is most important to keep the reverence for My Real Presence in the Host. My Commandments and My love never change. Be forewarned, when your Church leaders want to change My laws to accommodate evil practices in relaxing the sins of the flesh. These sins still are serious and need to be forgiven in Confession. This is why you will need to follow My Remnant Church, since many false shepherds will mislead the people. Keep with the traditional teachings of My Apostles and you will find eternal life. Do not let the Antipope lead you astray, as he will be in league with the Antichrist."

Later, at Adoration, I was seeing the altar of a Church with no statutes, the tabernacle was missing, and there was a modern cross of Resurrection. Jesus said, *"My people, it is reverence and thanksgiving that I desire from you before My Blessed Sacrament. You have pictures and mementoes all around your house for the love of your relatives. Should you not have statues or images of Me, My mother and the saints on the walls of your churches? The Crucifix with My suffering Body on it should be present on all the altars to remind you of the sacrifice I had to undergo for your sins. See, by these means of reverence, that you are acknowledging Me in public before My Father. Without this affirmation of your love for Me, how can I prove your love is sincere? Follow My Will for you and live My message of love in all you do for both love of God and neighbor."*

Saturday, July 5, 1997:

After Communion, I could see Mary in a beautiful array of light and she was in a grotto. Before me was a beautiful icon of St. Bernadette Soubirous kneeling at Lourdes. Mary said, *"My dear children, this is my celebration and acknowledgment of my Immaculate Conception. The significance, at this time, is that of your National Shrine as you celebrate your independence. This revelation to my daughter was to give witness to you of how blessed I was through the grace of God not to have any blemish of sin. To house the Babe of my Son, Jesus, in my womb, it had to be a perfect tabernacle of love to receive Him, unstained and perfectly free of any earthly defect. I was prepared for my mission as Mother of God from the moment my Son, Jesus, was promised as a Redeemer for all of mankind. This is why my Immaculate Conception is a glorious title to be guarding your nation. It is pointing all of you to seek to be heavenly perfect to receive your Lord. It should remind you also to go frequently to Confession, so you may be in the state of grace when you receive my Son in Holy Communion."*

Later, at Adoration, I could see the towers of St. James' Church in Medjugorje and I sensed Mary's presence. Mary said, *"My dear children, I am calling all of my little ones forward that you may properly make your consecration to me for the coming Feast of My Assumption on August 15. You will need this spiritual preparation for the events not long after this. Do not grow lax in your prayers this summer, since you need to be more focused on my Son than ever. During these coming trials, you will need the help of your angels as well. Pray to my Son, Jesus, and your guardian angels so you will be familiar to call on them in your need. You have been graced with a time of mercy. Do not waste this precious time on frivolous things. Thank you for listening to my call."*

Sunday, July 6, 1997:

After Communion, I could see out into the darkness of space at a small dot of light. Jesus said, *"My people, I am showing you in vision how small the Earth is in all of My creation. Even though you are witnessing scenes from Mars, man is but a spec in space. As you look out among the stars, your solar system is just one of these specs of light. How then do you think you can do anything without My help? Everything you have received in goods and talents, they all come from Me. The sooner man realizes that he cannot do anything on his own, then he will come to Me for help. When you give yourself over to My Will, then I can mold you into the person I have made you to be. By the fact that you are a creature in My creation, it means that you must praise your God and give thanks for all I have given you. I love each of you and you are not forgotten among all of these worlds. I am King of the Universe and you need to respect your God and give Me homage.*

Think of Me whenever you are boasting of any good fortune or accomplishment."

Later, at Adoration, I could see a light bulb go on and it symbolized having the idea to be seeking Jesus at all times. Jesus said, *"My people, many have been enjoying the fruits of My love in their lives. Still others are just now coming to know their Lord and the beauty of My love for them. It is sad for Me when men fail to understand My existence, or they are not even seeking a higher authority in their lives. To know and love Me, it is necessary to think beyond yourselves and ask why you are here. Too many souls are caught up in the pleasures and cares of this world to understand how finite your time is here. It is when you look beyond yourselves that you see My existence. It is understanding Creation and its beauties that you are led to know the Creator. This becomes a gift of faith that leads you to My love. When you receive Me in Communion or are before My Blessed Sacrament, you can drink in a full measure of My love. It is then that I share My Heavenly graces and blessings with you. Those who know Me, let Me lead their lives and they are filled with the joy that their salvation is assured. So pray, My children, for those far away from Me, so that they can enjoy the promise of living with Me in Heaven as well."*

Monday, July 7, 1997:

After Communion, I could see some rocks at the base of a mountain. Jesus said, *"My people, there are many places that are celebrated as places of My Presence. In the Old Testament, Mt. Sinai was holy ground where Moses had to remove his sandals. Today, with My Coming in My Sacramental Presence of the Host, all of your tabernacles are sacred places. In the time of the tribulation there will be special places of My holy ground as well. For at these places of apparition and holy ground, the angels will protect you where the luminous white crosses will be located. In every age I watch over My people in a unique way with My Presence."*

Later, at Adoration, I could see an older pastor looking dejected because of the parishioners who wanted a modern Church teaching instead of following Rome. Jesus said, *"My dear priest sons, it is not easy to deal with all of the many thoughts of those in a local parish. There are many interests and desires of those wishing to have their way in My Church. It is most important that My priests be spiritual leaders in their own congregations. Even though it is easier to go along with a majority opinion, it is more important to be willing to hold up My Gospel teachings as the more appropriate way of life. Do not be afraid to stand up for the teachings of My true Church, even when it is not popular. My priests are to represent Me on Earth, so be daring to preach as I would teach. Do not be so worried about the collection box as you should be concerned about saving the souls under your care. To feed your people properly, be willing to bring the people closer to the sacraments for their spiritual strength. When occasions arise, speak out on the problems of the lack of morals of this day. Speak out to wake them up to their sins and how they need to be forgiven in Confession. Those priests, who truly imitate My life in prayer and duty, will find true love in following My Will."*

Tuesday, July 8, 1997:

After Communion, I could see some stones when the devil tempted Jesus to make them into bread. Jesus said, *"My people, when I was tempted by the devil to provide food, I told him, 'Man does not live by bread alone, but according to the Word of God.' I have told you in many ways 'What does it gain you, to have acquired the whole world and then lose your soul?' It is important to keep everything in perspective. I give you many gifts in this life to help you and your neighbor, but do not live for these things only. You need to see that following My Will is your only road to perfection. Consecrate your whole life to Me, and I will provide for your every need. Faith and trust in Me are all that you need in life. See that I am the Living Bread that has come down from Heaven. I give Myself to you as a Heavenly Manna to take and eat. This spiritual nourishment will provide you with all the strength that you will need to reach Heaven."*

Later, at Adoration, I could see a Chinese man with a symbol of the hammer and sickle and he carried a sword over a huge globe of the Earth. Jesus said, *"My people, you are familiar with the symbol of the dragon as representing China. Having the largest population and a huge army under Communism, China will play a large role in the events coming upon the Earth. As you see in this vision, China will make its presence felt all over the world. You will see the powers of evil will use this force to its own advantage. Any coming wars in Asia and Europe will be influenced by China. These words are mentioned for your instruction and not for you to be fearful. I have told you many times to trust in My strength and not to worry what man can do. You will have wars and rumors of wars before the tribulation comes. The Antichrist will exploit these forces to control the world. Be ever in prayer, My faithful, since your spiritual strength will be required of you. Have peace in your heart since My power will be ever victorious."*

Wednesday July 9, 1997:

After Communion, I could look down into a deep well as the future source of water to drink. Jesus said, *"My people, the passage of Joseph in the Old Testament, which you have read today, is your sign of the end days. I have given this message of the coming famine many times, but today understand that even your drinking water will be scarce. This is why I have asked you to store food and water during your time of plenty. As in the time of Joseph, you will again experience a world famine. The Antichrist will use this food shortage to try and control the people through their buying and selling. My faithful have nothing to fear, since as Joseph saved and provided the food, I will provide you with a ration of My Heavenly Manna at the proper time. Do not succumb to the mark of the Antichrist, but follow My angels to the refuge where My angels will give you Spiritual Communion with the Bread of Angels. I love all of My people so much. Rest assured that I will watch over you and protect your souls from the evil ones. With faith and full trust in Me I will provide for your every spiritual and physical need."*

Thursday, July 10, 1997:

After Communion, I could see a long narrow cave and it opened up into a broad open section. Jesus said, *"My son, do not be afraid to go forth in talking of caves as protection in the time of persecution. There has been much precedence of such protection even in My Scriptures. It is important to see this means as one of the many ways I will be watching over My remnant. My angels will walk before you in leading you to places of safety from the evil one. Much like I protected My mother from any harm, I will protect your souls as well in the tribulation. You will face many hardships in the tribulation, but with My help and the shortened time, you will be saved. Have faith and trust in Me and you will live to see My day both in Heaven and on Earth."*

Later, at the prayer group, I could see some $10 and $20 bills and then a lovely mural on the floor of a Church. Jesus said, *"My people, some are torn between chasing after money or coming to kneel in Church to give praise and adoration to God. To those who adore money, you are following the gods of this world. Those who suffer the love of money, must come to realize that they need to know the Creator of everything through My grace. Store your true treasures in Heaven. This earthly treasure will fly from you tomorrow."*

I could see the top of an attic in Belgium where a cross was protecting this home. Jesus said, *"My people, I call you to consecrate your houses to My Sacred Heart. This is a powerful protection for your home, more than man could provide. The home is where your heart lies, for it is special for every family. Treat your home as a holy place through this consecration. Then My protection will be close to your family."*

I could see Mary come and she said, *"My dear children, I am grateful for your rosaries this evening. Your great faith in me and my Son will be your salvation. I have touched all of you with many blessings. These flakes, I have shown you before, are a blessing of my presence. Continue to pray much for the sinners of the world who are far from God."* (Several physical flakes were found on the floor in the pews.)

I could see a dove representing the Holy Spirit. The Holy Spirit said, *"I am the Spirit of Love and I come to bless you, My son, for your coming presentation Saturday. You have asked for My help at all of your talks and I will continue to inspire your words so the people will hear what they need to know at this time. Be ever vigilant in prayer, and the power of God will fill your heart with the great love We wish you to share with all of those listening to your words. No matter how much you will be tested, I will always be there to help you. It is your confidence and faith in God that will come across to these people."*

I could see a turnstile at a Carmelite monastery. I then saw St. Therese coming to give the message. St. Therese said, *"My son, I come in love to thank you for witnessing to me in your coming talk on the saints. It is good for you to remember these beautiful messages, so the people can see how much we in Heaven seek to bring you earthly souls to God. Imitate our lives, since all the saints had a burning love for God while we were on Earth. We could not do enough for Jesus. Cast your own wills aside and come to the service of your Lord. All that you do for Him will be multiplied in the blessings that He will pour out on you. The closer you come to live in His Divine Will, the more perfect you will grow in His love. Show your love for Him constantly, for He draws you to His heart of infinite love at all times."*

I could see some large piles of lumber for building in some woods. Jesus said, *"My people, you have been advised that many detention centers are being set up all over your country. These are places connected with the UN occupational forces throughout your country. Truly, now the One World forces are even moving their operations into your national parks. All of this should be no surprise, since I told you Satan's agents are preparing for the coming of the Antichrist. Fear not, My people, as evil will be great, My power over evil will be greater. Your protection from the demons will be carried out by My angels."*

I could see some missiles and other signs of man's advances in technology. Jesus said, *"My people, do not pride yourselves on all of these events taking place on Mars. Many praise man's accomplishments, but few recognize that it is through My gifts of knowledge that you can do anything. Also, in viewing these planets, you are just scratching the surface of the knowledge of My creations. As you understand more the workings of the universe, how can you not come to a deeper appreciation of My power and give Me the glory you should be giving Me?"*

Friday, July 11, 1997:

After Communion, I could see a pyramid representing a history of evil in Egypt. Jesus said, *"My people, as you read of My people, Israel, going to Egypt because of the famine, see how I use evil for good. Even though the Egyptians were idol worshipers, I showed through the plagues and other miracles how My power saved My people beyond that of men. The powers of evil have no hold on Me, nor will they corrupt your souls. I brought My people, Israel, out of Egypt's power as I will save you from the power of the Antichrist. The One World people have adopted this pyramid symbol as a sign of evil power. Do not fear even these monied people, for their strength will be stripped from them when I come in triumph. All power resides in Me, so there is nothing for you to fear. Trust in Me, as did My people of old, and I will bring you through your trial as well."*

Later, at Adoration, I could see a little town with an older wooden church. Jesus said, *"My people, look to my tabernacles where you will find My glorious Real Presence. It does not matter the size of the church or the number that attends. All that is important is that I am there for each of you. Give Me reverence in the way you receive Me in Holy Communion and before My Presence in My Blessed Sacrament. This bread I have consecrated through the priest's hands is My gift of love to you. When you are united with Me in My One Body, you have a little glimpse of what Heaven is all about. Those who are loyal to Me, I show the way to evangelize souls to Me. You always will need a strong prayer life to go with your mission. When I ask you to follow Me, it is to give up your will and the desires for worldly things. See the beauty of My graces and blessings on those who seek Me, for this becomes more of a burning desire to be with Me. You suffer through this earthly existence, but My reward of eternal life is beyond anything you could attain by yourselves. I give eternal life freely to all those who love Me and follow My commands. Relish the joy of when you will be with Me in the eternal rest of Heaven. You, My son, know this treasure and you need to share this experience with all of My faithful who will listen."*

Saturday, July 12, 1997:

At St. Francis Xavier Church, Petoskey, Minnesota, after Communion, I could see Jesus' face gradually materializing. Jesus said, *"My people, I am showing you this vision of My face in this way, because many do not recognize where I am. I have told you many times that where two or more pray in My Name, I am there in your midst. In each person you meet, you are seeing Me in the image I have made them. Even more, remember My Real Presence in the Host in your tabernacles. Do not forget to visit Me so you can adore and praise Me. For all I have given you, you need to give Me thanks. I rejoiced when the one cured leper returned to give Me thanks. Even more will I rejoice when you too, give Me thanks. My love is poured over you through My Presence. See this gift I have given you in My Eucharist and be ever joyous every time that you can receive Me. You will see abundant graces come over you for being faithful to My call to follow Me."*

Later, at the Smith's Marian Center, Petoskey, Minnesota, before the Blessed Sacrament, I could see a wedding banquet with the love of a young couple in the middle. Jesus said, *"My son, as you share these love messages with the people, I wish to share My personal love with all of you present. When you think about My love, it is like that of a newly married couple. To fully appreciate this love, try to extend this human love to an infinite level. Then you will be just touching the surface of My love. Again, when you think of My unconditional love, picture someone slapping Me in the face every day until their dying day. If that person would even think of Me, I still would have mercy on their soul. Your frequent sins are just like this slap in the face. Be sorrowful for your sins and come seek the grace of My forgiveness. See, My people, that you all are loved so much that I never give up on any soul, even if they be far from Me. You are the ones that limit My love. The more open your heart is, the more of My graces I will share with you. Constantly fight this battle for souls, since this is what true love in the Spirit is all about."*

Sunday, July 13, 1997:

At St. Francis Xavier Church, Petoskey, Minnesota, after Communion, I could see Our Lady coming off an altar with a flowing mantle as at Medjugorje. Then I could see a vision of the Marian Center. Mary said, *"My dear son, I come on this day to encourage all of my children to hold my consecration dear to their hearts. This is the day to start the preparation for my feast day on August*

15. The 13th is a special day for me as well at many of my places of apparition. I want to share with you the love I have for my blessed daughter, Barbara, for all the beautiful work she is doing for me and my Son. In many ways I have shown you how I bring souls to Jesus through me. When you have devotion to me, you see Jesus always in my arms. Our Two Hearts are joined as one. In all of the beautiful work that is being done, the search for saving souls through evangelization is key in your battle with the evil one. Do not forget to summon the help of Heaven with all of the angels and saints. Show God's love to all who will come forward to accept Jesus as their Savior. My love goes out to all of my children and I throw my mantle of protection around all who love me and my Son."

Later, before the Blessed Sacrament, I could see swords in an arc and they were piercing the heart of Mary as Our Sorrowful Mother. Mary said, *"My dear children, you are seeing me in deep sorrow, for I am crying because so many souls will not even recognize or even want to know my Son. So many souls have been seduced by the evil one with the pleasures and cares of the world. How is it that even with so many of my messages and miracles given at my apparition sites, still many do not want to believe. They have seen my Son die on the Cross and He was Resurrected from the dead, but still they will not believe. It is my faithful souls who lift up my spirit for doing my Son's Will. I must rely on all of my sons and daughters to go out and evangelize the lost souls of this age. I beckon my army to go out at double speed and with an intense spirit to bring souls to my Son quickly. You do not have much more time to save the souls of this age. Do not waste time, but do all in your power to work to save souls. Through prayer, good works, and your example in life, strive to save souls with a fervor of love in all of your actions. Seek your heavenly help in me, my Son and all the saints and angels. You will need our help in this desperate hour."*

Monday, July 14, 1997:

At Adoration. I could see some stars made by the children and Jesus was pleased with their work. Jesus said, *"My people, the young children are a joy to Me since their innocence leads them to Me.*

It is important that the children be taken to Mass to share in the knowledge of My love. Those parents who refuse to take their children to Mass, will face a strong judgement in My eyes. The little ones seek Me and if you thwart this natural inclination, you will get more stripes than for not going alone. The children are precious to Me. Do not abuse them or keep them from Me. The love of a child is so beautiful because of the full trust, they place in their parents. Do not destroy this trust, but imitate the children by placing your full trust in Me. By this innocent and trusting love, I call on you to become as little children in loving Me. Discard all of your worldly distractions and come to Me in blind trust so I may bring all of My children to their eternal salvation."

Tuesday, July 15, 1997:

After Communion, I could see various flowers as insignias for the people of power. Jesus said, *"My people, those in authority carry a heavy responsibility with them for those under them. Your leaders are called to a high moral order because of their position. If these leaders abuse their leadership and misdirect those under their charge, then surely they will be tested by My justice. In the readings, I condemned many of the towns of Israel for all of their abuses of My Commandments. The evil leaders of your day will meet the same fate as those people in Sodom. Do not think today's injustices will go unanswered. There will come a time when My angels will chain all of the demons and evil people in Hell for their evil deeds. Let this be an example to you, that all those, who flaunt My laws, will pay for their deeds in the end. It is your decision to be either with Me or against Me. There will be no middle ground of those giving lip service. I will come to separate the goats from the sheep. Listen to My commands of love and you will have your reward with Me in Heaven."*

Later, at Adoration, I could see Jesus get up and rise from the tomb. Jesus said, *"My people, I am the victor over death, over sin, and over Satan. There is nothing powerful enough to restrain Me. I do the Will of My Father because We are one in the same being. When you worry about the coming tribulation, do not give more credit to the power of evil than they deserve. All power and action resides in Me. I allow evil to exist in order to test your faith. If everything was done for you, there would be no testing of your love for Me. This is the good that comes from evil, so you can understand how beautiful it will be to live in My Divine Will. When you see the goal of being with Me forever, how can you not strive to do everything to please Me? Come follow Me in My footsteps so when you die, you also will be resurrected with Me in Heaven. Have no fear and believe always in My power which is much greater than any other power in the world."*

Wednesday, July 16, 1997:

After Communion, I saw a part of a house in the foreground and then a vision of some clouds way off into the distance of the horizon. Jesus said, *"My people, you are seeing in this vision how Moses was to direct the Israelites from their place in bondage to the clouds over Mt. Sinai. This is the same command that I am asking many of My messengers in leading the people of this age into the wilderness. In those days, it was to get away from the enslavement of the Egyptians. In these days, it will be to get away from the enslavement of the Antichrist, the bankers, and other One World agents. This is again a battle of good and evil and it is important to choose the right side of good at this time. Soon I will come to judge the good and the bad, but for now I have let you co-exist. At the time of the harvest of souls, I will gather the wheat into My barn, but the tares will be gathered to be burned in the fire of My justice. Prepare now, My children, for your time of judgment is near."*

Thursday, July 17, 1997:

After Communion, I could see a pentagon shape and it was brown colored. Jesus said, *"My people, you have seen the might of arms that have held up many great nations as the armaments of Egypt. Yet, when My people needed to be freed from Egypt's grasp, their arms meant nothing. When God's miracles were worked, all of Egypt's army and its arms were destroyed for violating God's Will. Today, you rely on the arms of your own defense to protect you and even bully nations to do your will. Many nations, who depended on their arms, have gone to ruin. Your nation has been greatly blessed, but now a moral decadence has befallen you and these arms, that you have, will not protect you. Many nations have fallen from within. Your nation, because of its sins and disregard for My laws, will fall as well. Your arms will be stripped from you by ruthless traitors and all that you depended on for strength will be brought low. The morals of your people are reflected in your leaders. I have protected your nation while you were faithful. Now, that you have turned your back on Me in your abortions and sins of the flesh, you will soon see your own demise. Unless you change your ways, you will go the way of destruction that I foretold for many sinful cities that I condemned in Israel. All the prosperity, that you have, comes from Me. When you violate My Will, it is just a matter of time until your fall is completed. Look to your future, America. If you do not heed My warnings, you will reap the whirlwind of destruction at your own hands."*

Later, at the prayer group, I could see an adult and there was a hand on a small tricycle with a child on it. At the bottom of the tricycle there were flames. Jesus said, *"My people, many of My little ones are in an evil environment which could lead their souls away from Me. My dear parents and grandparents, I want you to watch over and protect your children from the evils of this world. Do not stand by passively and allow My little ones to be snatched by the powers of Hell."*

I could see a parent placing a safety belt around a young child in their car seat. Jesus said, *"My dear parents, you abide by the laws of man to protect your children from being injured or killed. So I ask you now to be even more concerned for the spiritual lives of My children. Put on their Scapulars and give them Rosaries so they will have spiritual protection. Have faith in Me by praying to watch over the children to protect them from evil."*

I could see a yellow cross among the railings of a pleasure boat. Jesus said, *"My children, many of you spare no expense on your vacations and leisure time. All of your luxuries can be distractions from having a good prayer life. If you are so afraid to leave them, you could be dependent on them. You must come to Me stripped of all idols that may lead you away from Me. Come to Me in simple love and I will forgive you and lead you in carrying your cross of life. You will always be tested by trials. Come to*

Me and I will grant you My peace."

I could see someone comfortable in a lounge chair and then in a hammock. Jesus said, *"My people, it is not necessary to always be in comfort. You will be tested in many ways in life that will test your faith. The everyday tasks and challenges of each day must be suffered. Seek My help in your trials and expect that you will suffer persecution for My Name's sake. Satan and those who love the world will test you often. You must be ready and prepared with prayer to endure your daily testing. Always imitate My life and do not seek the comforts of the world."*

I could see Jesus washing the feet of the Apostles. Jesus said, *"My dear people, if you would be great in Heaven, you must serve the rest. My souls in the world are being attacked by Satan and his demons. I am asking all of My faithful to serve in evangelizing the lost souls. Many souls do not realize the danger their souls are in because your society has grown more evil over time. These messages are being sent as a wake-up call to those souls far from Me. My children, invite these souls to My love and encourage them with your good example."*

I could see a boot of a soldier about to step on our soil. Jesus said, *"My people, there are many foreign troops training in your country. They are about to march soon to take over your country. Your defenses are being stripped from you by the One World people. These powerful people will allow your country to fall to these foreign UN troops. Many of you are too trusting and do not realize how close you are to having your freedoms removed. Your religious persecution will come swiftly. Pray for My protection in this tribulation and My angels will protect you. Fight only with your spiritual weapons, for guns cannot fight these evil powers."*

I could see Mary coming in a blue dress with a calm, loving face. Mary said, *"My dear children, thank you for your many Rosaries tonight. I will raise up your prayers to my Son for your petitions. Because of your prayers, I will raise up Australia before my Son as well. People of Australia, listen to my requests. By the power of your Rosaries, you will hold up my mantle of protection against the evils of your land. If there is not enough prayer, you will lessen my protection. So pray my three Rosaries each day and say my consecration prayers, so all of your souls may be close to my Son's Heart. Seek His love, my children, and all else will be given you."*

Friday, July 18, 1997:

After Communion, I could see a circular piece of unleavened bread followed by a figure that looked like Moses carrying a staff in flight. Jesus said, *"My people, with today's readings you are familiar with the customs of My people in Israel on Passover. But it was this same time that I became the Lamb of God, offered up for your sins. Now, there is a new Passover where man has been set free from his bondage to sin. Pharoah released My people as I have released you. Heaven is now open to those who follow Me. In days past, the people celebrated with the matzah to commemorate the Passover, since the manna was given from Heaven. Now, I give you a Living Bread in My Presence in the Eucharist, which is truly your spiritual manna from Heaven. In your coming tribulation, you will see the use of My manna once again will feed you from Heaven. In addition to your physical sustenance, you will be given My Real Presence in your spiritual sustenance as well. This miracle of Bread from Heaven was shown to you in the witness you visited previously. Be assured that I will watch over My remnant and I will feed you when you call on Me in your need."*

Saturday, July 19, 1997:

At Church (Andrea's wedding), after Communion, I could see shimmering blue water reflections on the sides of a Church. I then saw a curtain open and there was a large ring present. Mary came and said, *"My dear children, the blue water you are seeing is to remind you of your Baptism. This was your first entry into the Church and your first encounter with my Son. See in this wedded love, a reflection of my Son's love for all of you in His Church. You all are the bride of my Son, since He first created you in His image. Each day your faithfulness to my Son is tested. The vows of marriage are a covenant between the bride and the groom. As God the Father made a covenant with Moses in the Ten Commandments, my Son fulfills this covenant by dying for your sins. You all are called to be God's people. It is your response to say 'I do' in knowing, loving, and serving God. A true covenant is made when both parties abide by the agreements reached. Jesus loves you infinitely. It is your duty to return his love and thank Him for all the many gifts of life, faith and creation. You can show your love with a devout prayer life. Live to please Jesus in all of your actions."*

Later, at Nocturnal Adoration, I could see Jesus crucified on His cross and it appeared that He was suffering on every corner of the street at every block. Jesus said, *"My people, I have died once and for all men's sins, past, present, and those in the future. You are seeing Me suffer on every street corner to show you that I suffered for all men. This thought is to confront you, so you will not make Me suffer more when you change your desire to sin less. Every time you sin, you are like those at My scourging giving Me an extra stripe. This scene is to make it vivid to you how much grief each sin causes Me. I seek all of you to be sorrowful for all of your many insults to Me, and you need to seek My forgiveness in Confession. Now, you need to come to Me no matter how evil you think you are. For I will accept anyone who wishes to convert and imitate My life."*

Sunday, July 20, 1997:

After Communion, I could see inside a dark pit. People were in the pit reaching up for someone to pull them out. Jesus said, *"My people, as I look out over the Earth, there are many souls crying out for help, but Satan has a hold on many of them. Many souls are so in love with the world that they do not even notice My call. These souls will be condemned, unless someone brings Me to them. Other souls have heard Me, but even in My Church they are being misled by false witnesses. My dear faithful remnant, you do not know how fortunate you are to know and love Me. Those who have accepted My Will are a joy to My Heart. It is this core of believers that I call on, to go out and evangelize the lost souls of the world. The time for saving these souls is short, and unless they are given a hand out of their sin, they will remain in the darkness. Come, My children, your Father is calling all souls to His bosom. Help these poor souls while there is still time for conversion. You must work in haste and without regard for criticism. Souls are at stake, so you must act quickly."*

Later, at Adoration, I could see a spiritual outline of an angel that looked like St. Michael the Archangel. I asked Jesus' permission for him to speak. St. Michael said, *"I am ever watchful for those who call on me for protection from the demons. For those in doubt, there is a real angel called Satan. It is only by God's power that I am allowed to rebuke him and other demons. Do not think that Satan's power could ever threaten the power of God. The demons are allowed to tempt man, but God always allows heavenly power to be available to hold evil in check. You will not be overpowered by evil, but you will empower it only through your acceptance by your free will. Therefore, when you meet any trial, call on us angels to fight your battle for you. We are ever present to help you. Give glory to God by trusting in our help. If you focus on Jesus at all times, you will not even afford Satan the opportunity for sin. It is only when you yield to the desires of the flesh, that sin can take hold of you. If you keep a prayerful life, you will be able to endure these temptations, no matter how often they occur. Call on my name or Jesus in fighting the demons at any time. We will come rushing to your aid and turn aside these evil ones. You need to be aware of evil's existence, but do not give credit for any power to the evil ones. Jesus' power is so overwhelming that when His Name is mentioned, it is enough to rout the demons."*

Monday, July 21, 1997:

After Communion, I could see some large rocks. Then I saw a pyramid emerging from the ground. Jesus said, *"My people, you are constantly seeing a power struggle between men over goods, land, and money. At times it is open warfare, and at other times it means a political takeover. You have seen drug lords, kings and dictators throughout history. Sometimes it is only through death that these forces are removed. Hidden behind these power struggles is a constant battle of good and evil. Remember that My power reigns supreme and that whatever forces man has brought about, I have crumbled. Never fear any evil force, since over time it will be brought low. There is no lasting power in man, since I am the eternal power which everyone must answer*

to. Believe in Me and you will see My power in your life lead you over seemingly impossible obstacles. Soon My triumph will sweep throughout the whole Earth."

Later, at Adoration, I could see a large flaming abyss that seemed to have no bottom. Many souls were falling into Hell. Jesus said, *"My dear children, My mother and I are both sorrowing for how many souls are being lost in Hell. My children, you must realize how serious it is to lose your soul to the evil one. Eternity in Hell is an eternal banishment from My sight and a severe and painful suffering forever. All of this is because those souls refused to accept Me as Lord of their lives. Your selfishness and desire of earthly things can bring you to this place of torment. My children, you must struggle to stop your abortions and your sins of the flesh. If you do not convert your lives, you will meet with this fate of eternal punishment in Hell. Reach out to those lost souls and plead with them, if you could only bring them to*

Me. Let them come to eternal love with Me and not eternal hate from Satan. How many times must I seek you to bring you to your senses. Your sins bring you a false pleasure for a short time. But you are trading a brief satisfaction for an eternity of grief. Think of how long eternity is. You think in terms of a number of years, but how can you imagine a number with an infinite number of zeroes? If you had time to live all the lives of everyone that existed, it would not even scratch the surface of eternity. So come to Me now, My children, and seek My forgiveness of your sins. See eternal beauty and love with Me far surpasses any thought of being with the hideous faces of the demons and their hate for you. Choose life and you will be forever with the light. Choose death and you will curse the darkness forever."

Tuesday, July 22, 1997: (St. Mary Magdalene)
After Communion, I was looking up out of a grave. Gradually, I was rising up out of the grave. Jesus said, *"My people, I am the Resurrection and the Life. No one can come to the Father except through Me. All of you are appointed to die because of Adam's sin, but you have been promised redemption because of My death on the Cross. Therefore, those who are faithful will be raised from the tomb into a glorious life with Me in Heaven. As you view yourself rising, all of My faithful will realize this dream, just as I have promised. I keep all of My promises. Each of you, that comes to Me, will share in the glory of My love and peace in Heaven. Do not be concerned with the pain of death, for I have conquered sin and death. I am pure love and when you rest with Me, your joy will be complete. Sharing with Me in Heaven is the fulfillment of My promise to each of you. Your life in the Spirit does not end with death, but it is a new beginning of life that you will enjoy forever. So have faith, My little ones. He, who gives up everything for Me, will reap a lasting reward that you cannot even comprehend."*

Later, at Adoration, I could see a holy water well at a Church entrance and some water was dripping into a pool. Jesus said, *"My people, it is good for you to know the power that I impart to those who bless themselves with holy water. This is one of My gifts that I have asked you to take into hiding. It needs to be blessed prop-*

J. Terelya

erly with the holy salt. It can be used in exorcisms and other times to protect yourselves from the demons. It is used by the priest to bless sacramentals. The blessing of the holy water is placed on any object with an intention of being prayed over. See that there is a measurable increment in the amount of energy between plain water and holy water. This blessing of holy water is a gift you will need soon in your protection during the tribula-

tion. Treasure every gift I give you, for its purpose is to ultimately, save your souls. This is a universal gift for everyone, but it is mostly understood through My remnant."

Wednesday, July 23, 1997:

After Communion, I could see a glorious display of the Baptism of Jesus in the Jordan with a miraculous presentation of the Trinity with God the Father and a bright white colored dove representing the Holy Spirit. Jesus said, *"My people, this mysterious display of the Blessed Trinity gives you many lessons. At the outset, it is one of the few places in Scripture where the Three Persons in One God are made manifest. This is so you can know to love the Father, the Son and the Holy Spirit as one. This also confirms the preaching of St. John the Baptist which was to repent and be baptized. You all need conversion in whatever place in life you find yourself. It is not enough to exist and support yourself, but you must find the true meaning of life by coming to Me as your Savior. See how I pour out My gifts of love and sustenance for your body and your soul. As you saw how I cared for My people in the desert, be ever trusting in Me to lead and provide for you. When you come to know Me, you will see that I am the Living Bread which you cannot survive without. See that I am the object of desire by every soul. Your souls seek My rest and they seek to be with their Creator. Give up your own will and see that your calling is to follow My Will to your eventual perfection."*

Thursday, July 24, 1997:

After Communion, I could see large ground antennae receiving communications from satellites and there were dark clouds over them. Jesus said, *"My dear people, how quickly you have come to embrace all of your new found technological communications. Many of your advances seem to give you outward advantages, but beware of the potential abuses of these new ways. Many of these public access lines will be monitored to control all of your calls and transactions. All of these electronic connections will no longer be protected. So, do not trust in man, but rather trust in God to lead you. When the evil one assumes power, all of these new advances will be used against you. Think soon that you will have to disconnect yourself with all of these electrical transmissions, since the Antichrist would control your mind. Plan now for your retreat into the wilderness for protection. Seek My help to guide you."*

Later, at the prayer group, I could feel Our Lady's presence very strong and I saw a little girl's eyes. Mary said, *"My dear children, I call on all of my younger and older faithful to come close to my heart. When you pray my Rosary and do my Son's Will, I reward you with many signs of my grace. Continue your prayers daily for my intentions."*

I could see the ends of many barrels of guns and rifles. Jesus said, *"My people, I rebuked St. Peter for raising arms to defend Me. It is good for you to remember that it is your prayers that will be your spiritual weapons. Do not raise up guns for fighting, since you offend me enough with your killings. Think to please Me with your heavenly bouquet of your prayers. This adoration pleases Me greatly."*

I could see some churches burning as they were being destroyed one after another. Jesus said, *"Yes, My people, the tribulation is coming soon. You will see the agents of the Antichrist burning the churches, as you will be forced into underground churches. Bear with this trial but a short time and you will receive your reward."*

I could see a football stadium with a very small crowd. Jesus said, *"My people, the Antichrist will lead the people to many stadiums at once to worship him. This will be his aspiration to have souls defy God and follow him. Over time, fewer and fewer people will give worship to the Antichrist because they will see that he is the father of lies. I will lead all of you to safety through My Cross. So have trust in Me that I will watch over you."*

I could see many beautiful buildings of large corporations. Jesus said, *"My people, many of your corporations lord it over My people to get as much money out of them as possible. All those employers who take advantage of their employees will have to answer to Me. They will reap bitter herbs instead of profits for those who worship profits before helping their employees. You workers must also give your employers a fair day's work for your pay. All of you have obligations to Me that must be kept."*

I could see some people with concrete mixers and they were building a new refuge. Jesus said, *"My people, many of you have been called upon to form refuges for the tribulation. Some have been given specific instructions what to build in order to house My people. Do continue on your path to help those who will need lodging in their fight against the Antichrist. This battle of good and evil is progressing to its completion."*

I could see some beams of wood holding up a basement floor. Jesus said, *"My people, do not fear this time of the tribulation, since I will be providing for you in a special way. Call on Me, and My angels will lead you to your destination. Many of you may have to suffer for a while in uncomfortable places. But have faith in My works to protect you. I will not abandon you, but I will lead you to places of refuge that you will be willing to share with the love of My remnant. It is my faithful that you will meet with big smiles and loving hearts. All of you will share in My common love where you will be protected."*

Friday, July 25, 1997: (St. James)

After Communion, I could see some important leaders of old. Jesus said, *"My people, do not seek to be famous or powerful in the eyes of the world. It cannot be so for My disciples. As I told My Apostles, if you wish to be great in the eyes of Heaven, you must serve the rest. I, also, came to serve My Father by dying for all of men's sins. All of My faithful must help in evangelizing souls. It is serving Me that is so important by helping the lost souls. By following My Will in this apostolate, that is how you will please Me the most. All of those, who do My Father's bidding, will surely be graced to be with us in Heaven. Be humble and seek the lowest places of honor at My banquet and I will come to tell you to move up higher. Let someone else seek your place for you and in humble submission you will gain everything. Seek My heavenly treasures in all of your spiritual aspirations."*

Later, at Adoration, I could see a large dark arrow pointing down over a large hole in the ground. Jesus said, *"My people, many times I have tried to alert you to the pitfalls of Satan and all of his lies. You alone are responsible for where your soul will eventually reside. It is by your choice in life as to whether you will fol-*

low My Will of love. My children, you must help one another to remain close to Me and avoid any earthly distractions. Your gift of faith is enough to save you, but you must keep your gaze fixed on Me. The road to Hell is full of good intentions. It is how you actually live and what you do with your life that will determine your destination. Come to Me, My children, and I will give you My rest. You will need perseverence in this evil day to keep your path to Me open and away from the sirens of this world. Be quick to save your souls and others, for time is growing short."

Saturday, July 26, 1997: (Sts. Anne & Joachim)

After Communion, I could see some chairs and open doors to a house. St. Anne came and said, *"If you truly want to save souls, you must be willing to pay the price to help them. All souls have a price, if they do not come to God on their own. Too often many complain that their prayers are not answered. They must realize that some sinners have a higher price and may require your actions and prayers for a long time. In these cases, do not become lazy, but persevere in seeking Heaven's help."*

Later, at Adoration, I could see some black helicopter gun ships in flight. Jesus said, *"My people, beware of the weapons of destruction of the Antichrist. These helicopters, that you are seeing, have a considerable amount of firepower that can threaten many into submission. They are even now mapping out the targets to first remove. These would be the people who could expose their plan for takeover. They also will be targeting those who would have either physical weapons or are religious enemies of the Antichrist. They are mapping out crowds and possible places to hide. These are in fact agents of the UN which the Antichrist will control. Have no fear, My children, for My angels will confound these evil men, making many of their weapons useless. Seek My power and do not fear any power of evil which is subject to My control. You will need My purification to rid all evil on the Earth. Pray for My judgment to come quickly to place the demons in Hell once again."*

Sunday, July 27, 1997:

After Communion, I could see a child's train of empty cars and then a family with younger children. Jesus said, *"My people,*

THE
LORD

the family is such an important part of your society. Yet, it has come under increasing attack by various evil forces. It is important that each person helps to strengthen the whole family. You all have been given many talents and you should use your talents to witness My glory. It is those, who waste their talents or who are selfish, that will have to answer to Me. It is the same in your spiritual family, that you should help one another to remain faithful to your Lord. All men are called in their souls to serve and love Me. Those faithful need to encourage the fallen away souls to come back to their Lord who loves them. The harvest of souls is great, but only a few have accepted this responsibility. See, My children, that the struggle to save souls from the evil one will be your most important task. Those who bring souls to Me will be greatly received in Heaven."

Later, at Adoration, I could see some crosshairs and there were some large shells standing upright, ready to be used. Jesus said, *"My people, there are war clouds gathering for another major conflict. How long to you think your prosperity will last? A few incidents later and men will be taking up weapons to fight another war for the One World interests. Whenever oil or money interests are at risk, your country's leaders are soon advised to mobilize because of what is at stake. You will soon see many countries drawn into a new conflict which no country really wants to win. But the One World people will encourage you to fight for them. When Satan has you eating out of his hand, you should know there is more to this plan than meets the eye. The evil one is always working on his next attack against your souls. Whenever he can get men to kill each other, he has won a battle. But you must pray for peace and refuse to go to war for these people. They collect the blood money for weapons and they win again when you retrieve their prize of money or oil."*

Monday, July 28, 1997:

After Communion, I could see a large eye with a brown pupil. Jesus said, *"My people, when you have the gift of sight, you have all of life open to you. But many abuse this gift and only use it to gain earthly desires. Then others look deeper into life and can see the hand of their Creator. When you use your eyes of faith, it is the spiritual context that puts life in full perspective. Learn to view things more as I would see them and you will gain in perfection. It truly is your outlook on life that directs how you will serve Me. Pray each day to be guided by the Holy Spirit in your actions and you will be able to follow My Will for you. It is this direction of following My Divine Will that will truly show you how to follow the light. When you use your gift of sight to follow your Lord, you will see your way to Heaven. That day when you come to Heaven, your eyes will be open to a splendor of My love that your soul forever seeks."*

Later, at Adoration, I could see a puddle of blood and water and Jesus was on the Cross. There was a constant dripping of blood and water. The puddle had spread out from the foot of the Cross on Calvary. Jesus said, *"My people, what you are seeing is a cleansing of the world's sin by My death on the Cross. My blood is being poured out even today for the sins of your age. All of you weigh heavy on My shoulders. I carry you as lambs on My shoulder until the day when you will come to Heaven. You have constant need of My cleansing graces in My Sacrament of Reconciliation. Come to Me often, so your soul can be cleansed and made radiant in My sight again. Do not wallow in your sins, but see the filth of sin around you and seek to be free. My graces are always open to you. All you have to do is reach out in prayer for Me and I will come to your aid. Many either feel unworthy to be forgiven or they are steeped in the pleasures of habitual sin. Pray for those souls who cannot break their habits long enough to look for Me. Do not let your hearts grow cold to Me, but lift them up to be saved. As long as you keep your eyes fixed on Me, I will bring you to your salvation. So hasten to make reparation and be ever before My Presence in My Eucharist."*

Tuesday, July 29, 1997: (St. Martha)

After Communion, I could see a cameo picture of Jesus' face among some furniture. Jesus said, *"My people, today, I wish to share with you in thanking all those who take time in welcoming Me and others into your home. There are many opportunities to help others in a short stay overnight or sharing a friendly meal. Those who provide the food and other comforts in the home have their day in the sun today for My blessing. In addition to sharing with others in your home, remember to always welcome Me in your gatherings as well. Grace at meals, crucifixes, or pictures of Me in your home show others that I am present in your hearts as well. This is a total loving picture where you are showing your love for God and neighbor. Continue to live with these high ideals in living life to the fullest. All of your service I have noted, as one day I will serve you, when I welcome you to your eternal stay with Me in Heaven."*

Later, at Adoration, I could see three colors with black around them. Then it became blurred as I was moving higher to see a high definition TV screen. Jesus said, *"My people, you need to be more aware of your new electronic devices. Many of your new TV's and computers have means for two-way communication. Some have ways to view and listen to you even when it is turned off. The One World people are making things ready for the Antichrist. All of their devious plans are to help him control this world. I have told you to be watchful. A time is coming, right before the Antichrist's coming, when you will have to get rid of all of your electrical devices. The Antichrist, by his powers of suggestion, will use your TV's to get you to worship him. This is why you will need to go into hiding to avoid any of his hold on you. Seek My help in all of this tribulation, for without Me, you will be lost. Trust Me, that My power will rule at all times. I will protect all of*

My faithful, but you will still have to suffer from persecution. Live for today and pray for what I will give you to do at the time of the trial. Endure this age but a moment, and soon you will have your reward in My Era of Peace."

Wednesday, July 30, 1997:

After Communion, I could see a veil placed over a monstrance and another veil over a tabernacle. Jesus said, *"My people, when My Presence was in repose in the Old Testament, a veil covered the Holy of Holies. So also, today you place a veil over My Blessed Sacrament. It is right to give My Blessed Sacrament a place of honor, but many churches have hid My Presence that many cannot see where it is. You also, should remember that My Blessed Sacrament is meant to be adored. Encourage your clergy to have Exposition frequently to share the many graces the people can have by even visiting My exposed Host. Also, give Me adoration and acknowledge My love as often as possible. You have the Kingdom of God present among you in My Real Presence. Give thanks to God for all the blessings that have been bestowed upon you."*

Thursday, July 31, 1997:

After Communion, I could see some crevices in a desert. Jesus said, *"My people, take a lesson from the Israelites in the desert who had such trust in their Lord to lead them. They would not go forward unless the cloud of the Lord moved. It will be like this with your own exodus experience when I will be physically leading My people once again through My angels. You, also, will treasure My Presence by enshrining My Eucharist. In all places with My Host, My angels will be protecting you. You will have to preserve your faith and My Blessed Sacrament from the threats of the evil ones. My help at that time will lead you through this coming trial. Continue to place your full trust in Me, for My power will overcome Satan and the Antichrist."*

Later, at the prayer group, I could see a tank driving around on city streets. Jesus said, *"My people, man has always tried to lord it over other men with his weapons. See, My people, that fighting and killing does not solve anything, but only makes roots for a future war. It is senseless killing in these acts of terrorism that causes further hatred for each other. If enough of these incidents occur, they will plant the seed of another war."*

I could see some bathers on the beach. Jesus said, *"Take care, My children, that you dress properly even in the heat of summer. Those who do not take care in their dress, may be causing sin in the hearts of weak souls around them. Many women by their actions and dress bring crimes of rape upon themselves. So do not be an occasion of sin for others by your indecent dress. Instead, imitate My mother in how she led a chaste life. It is possible to control your passions when you pray for heavenly help."*

I could see a man in a clothing shop and he was sitting asleep from drinking too much. Jesus said, *"My people, many have fallen victim to over indulging in their drinking. You must be careful, My children, not to let the troubles of the world drive you to drinking. Do not seek to lessen your problems through any substance abuse. When your problems seem to overwhelm you, turn to praying to Me to help you. Do not give in to despair, but remember that I am by your side ready to walk with you in carrying your cross. You may, at times, suffer as I did on My road to Calvary, but you must struggle to follow My Will."*

I could look out of a cave at some people dressed as Arabs and they were helping the Antichrist to rule over the people. Jesus said, *"You must be strong, My children, to endure the coming events of My purification. Many are anxious to know the dates of when this will occur. I have given you only signs as Jonah to describe the evil age that you are in. Be prepared in your souls for when I will come for you. By constant Confession, you will always be ready if your life is required of you. As you witness the signs of the End Times, you know your time of deliverance is near."*

I could see some lovers hiding at night in their sins of the flesh. Jesus said, *"Do not think, My people, that because you sin in secret, that I will not know of your fornications and other such sins of the passions. Grab hold of your senses and live properly as the saints give you models to follow. For every sin of lust, you will have to reckon with Me at the judgment. Believe that I know your every action and you will be thinking more to please Me by guarding your passions. Do not let your earthly desires control your soul. Instead, let your spirit work with Me to gain eternal life. Follow My Will and you will be with Me in Heaven. Pray to have a good prayer life, so you will be strong in the face of these temptations."*

I could see a golden glow of light on the people at an apparition site of Our Lady. Mary came and said, *"My dear children, this golden glow of my love will fall on all of my faithful at my apparition places. I pour out graces upon all pilgrims who take time to visit my shrines. Even my statues and icons are witnessing to my love. This gold on the icon of your home is a touch of my love on your house. It is a blessing that I give you for struggling to save souls when it is so difficult. Take this as a sign that I will hear and answer your prayers through my Son. Have faith in both Our Hearts and share this sign of Our love with others. All of these signs are to wake up sinners and show them that Heaven is watching and encouraging you."*

I could see some luxury cars grow in size. Jesus said, *"My people, many have grown rich in worldly possessions, but I look into the heart. If your intention is to gain riches for its own sake, you will come to your own ruin. See that these riches lure you only to seek even more. Men, drunk with a desire for money, will never find satisfaction here in this life. So do not worry or waste your lives to have all the money you can obtain. I am your God, so do not trust in money, but trust only in Me. I see the motives of your heart. Seek heavenly treasures and you will be satisfied. Use your money to help others and you will be rewarded in My love."*

Friday, August 1, 1997:

After Communion, I could see a river lapping up against the banks and the water was high as at flood stage. Jesus said, *"My dear children, you keep asking for signs and there are signs all around you. The testimony of your sins has been brought before Heaven many times. Is it any surprise to you that My chastisements have already begun on your land? I tell you, that you will be continuously tested by fire and water, until you have come to your knees seeking help from your God. How long do you think I could dismiss all that you are doing? Your actions are bringing your own fate about you. My son, do not be disturbed over any persecution that you must endure. You will be tested worse than what you have faced until now. So speak out on all that I have witnessed to you, that souls may be alerted and saved. Be faithful to your prayer life in all that you go through and I will help you on your path to Heaven."*

Later, at Adoration, I could see someone kneeling on some parched ground. Jesus was standing before them and His shadow shaded them from the sun. Jesus said, *"My people, I am always watching out for the safety of your soul. As this shadow shows you, some do not even realize how I protect you in many ways on Earth. As your need for help arises, seek to have My shadow of protection come between you and the heat of your problems. You will see many tests throughout life. It is up to you to seek My help. When you refuse My help, you fail to gain My graces and many times your trials lead you to the breaking point. I am here to alleviate your suffering, if you so choose. Why do you want to go it alone without my help? See that without Me, you will always be searching for peace in your soul. Those who let Me lead them, find consolation in My ways that are easier than your ways. You complicate life by loving other things than Me and you are too curious for things that you do not need to know. Come to Me in simple faith as a child of God, and you will find your rest in My infinite love."*

Saturday, August 2, 1997:

At Mission Viejo, California, before the Blessed Sacrament, I could see an icon of Mary from a distance and she was holding the Infant Jesus. Mary came and said, *"My dear child, I have shown you my gold icon. I have advised you to pray my consecration prayers. Now, my pilgrim statue of Fatima is at your step. All of these helps of mine are not a coincidence, but it is my motherly way of coming to help you in your time of need. Many of men's lives are hollow, chasing after the things of this world. But you are called to go forth and preach the love of my Son and me. Many have refused to listen to either of us, since their hearts are far from us. You must tell the people that the spiritual life of their souls is the most important priority in all they do. You see how much expense people go through to comfort the body, which is only here for eighty years or more. You should be vigilant in the planning of your life and spend your time bringing your soul to my Son, Jesus, in order to be saved. Look to your priorities in life and be willing to suffer the body's pains so your spiritual life is lifted up more than your physical life. Your soul will live for eternity. Is not your soul's destination the most important concern in this life? If so, then you may need to change many of your daily habits and put God back into your life more."*

Later, at Mass in Mission Viejo, California, after Communion, I could see Jesus coming with the New Jerusalem. Jesus said, *"My son, you are confused and worried at times of the words of Scripture. I have given you adequate explanations of the Scriptures of this coming Era of Peace. Do not be anxious, but be joyful that this era will come quickly. Those who have died, will truly never die again in their glorified bodies. Those who live through the tribulation and did not die, will live long lives in this New Jerusalem on Earth. The end of this present age will come with My purification. The end of the Era of Peace will be the Final Judgment. Do not be so concerned about how things will be. Only have trust and faith in My Words of the Scripture, that they all will be fulfilled in due time. You should share in My great joy and love that these events are about to take place."*

Sunday, August 3, 1997:

At the Serra Chapel, San Juan Capistrano, California, after Communion, I could see a glorious Mass in a large cathedral and then I saw a flow of ethereal graces flowing over the Communion rail. Jesus said, *"My dear people, the priest has given you in words what you should know for all time. My Death on the Cross was the supreme sacrifice that I have given all of you as a gift of My Real Presence among you. The Sacrifice of the Mass is that perpetuation of my Death in an unbloody manner. It is the Transubstantiation of the bread and wine by the words of the priest that brings My Real Presence upon these species of bread and wine made into My Body and Blood. This is why you must receive Me without mortal sin on your souls. Give respect for My Sacrament even in Adoration. This is the Miracle of My Presence that needs to be honored and respected. It is true that no other message, apparition, or locution will make Me any more present than My*

Real Presence that is already there. But it is to raise up the faith of My people that I have allowed such miracles of My grace. Prepare, My children, for soon the Mass will be taken away from you in public. You will need to seek the Mass underground and you will be left only with My mother's Rosary and your Bible. Preserve My Presence wherever it can be found. Guard over your souls during this trial and seek My help and that of My angels to protect you. They will guide you to where you will be safe in various refuges. I will not leave you unprotected, but you will need full trust in Me and My words of prophecy. Trust in the spirit of these words that I will be guarding your souls from evil. All I ask is that you be faithful in worshiping Me only. I am the God of the universe. You cannot have salvation unless you come through Me."

Monday, August 4, 1997:

After Communion, I could see someone bicycling on a dirt road in the rain. Jesus said, *"My people, you are seeing again how you may have to use bicycles in traveling to a place of hiding. You will see your angels leading you to many refuges back on dirt roads away from the cities. Two situations may cause you to use bicycles. First, many of your newer cars have transponders in them so the evil people may be able to track where you are. The other reason will be a shortage of gas for your car because of war in the Mid-East. Be ready, My children, to flee when My Pope John Paul II leaves Rome and when evil people will be placing the mark of the beast on people. Those that hesitate to leave at these signs, may risk capture in the detention centers. Have trust in Me and I will have your angels protect you. Do not fear, but have faith in My Word."*

Later, at Tom and Ann's prayer group I could feel a strong presence of Our Lady. I then could see a large river with beautiful lands on either side of the river. Mary said, *"My dear children, those of you who live out away from the cities share with me in the love of nature. You see the beauty of creation, yet it is here that it may be a safe haven for many from evil people. You all are very dependent on your electricity for your comforts. You would do well to live without these comforts. It would be better for your souls if you returned to rural living on the farm. Without your fast style of life, you would have more time for God."*

Tuesday, August 5, 1997:

After Communion, I could see some large doors swing open by a beach. Jesus said, *"My people, I do so much for you everyday. Why do you keep your cold stony hearts closed to My love? If you do not open your hearts to My love, how can I enter to give you My rest? Once you let Me gain access to your heart, I will help you in cleaning out your excess baggage. In order for Me to mold you to My Will, it is necessary to do some spiritual spring cleaning. You have to empty yourself of so much pride and self-love, before I can replace that with My love and that of your neighbor. You must cleanse the sins of darkness that hold you captive. Let Me come into your heart and free you of all of your fears. Then My joy and peace can be infused into you, so all of life will come alive for you. You have to take charge of your life and ask for My help. Then I will move you with a burning desire to go out and help others. You cannot hold My love just within you. It needs to be shared with everyone. Do not be afraid to reach out with a helping hand, but let My Spirit move you to do it out of love for Me. You will see that once you accept My ways all of your inhibitions to be more open in your love will disappear. Rejoice in My Words of the Gospel to go out and preach My love to all men."*

Later, at Adoration, I could see some windshields of various cars. Then I saw rain being removed from the windshields by the wipers. Jesus said, *"My people, I am showing you in life what the forgiveness of sin is all about. You live in the world, but are not of the world. See how the rain is likened to the evil of the world that falls on you in your car. The windshield wipers are symbolic of how you are cleansed and made clean. Temptations and sin are always dropping on your windshields, but you must seek My Sacrament of Reconciliation in order to be forgiven by Me in the priest. Keep your soul always clean and in sanctifying grace and you will see clearly both at night or day. In some of the visions, it is not always clear what is being said or seen. In this case, there is an obvious analogy being used. So use My Sacrament of Reconciliation to remain clean, no matter how often you call on it. I will always forgive a repentant sinner. Be not afraid of any penance you will need to do. Just come in love and I will greet you with open arms."*

Wednesday, August 6, 1997: (Transfiguration)

After Communion, I saw a bookcase with three openings. I then was given a presence of the Trinity and the vision of a dove representing the Holy Spirit. Jesus said, *"My people, My Transfiguration was to give added faith to My Apostles before they received the Holy Spirit in tongues. It also was to help them understand when I would be Resurrected. Accounts in the Scriptures do not give witness to the Holy Spirit's Presence, but He was there just the same. Wherever I am, you also see My Father as well as the Holy Spirit. We are Three Persons in One God, so We cannot be thought of as separate beings — We are all in One. The understanding of the Holy Spirit had not yet been revealed, so this account did not include the Holy Spirit, but His evidence was still there. The Blessed Trinity is a mystery for you to understand, as is the understanding of God. We reveal Ourselves through Scrip-*

ture so that you know We rule the Heavens and the Earth. All creation must answer to Us as servants. We do not force Our love on you because of your free will, but We are reaching out to your heart to be ever one with Us."

Thursday, August 7, 1997:

After Communion, I could see a large hollowed out cave and then an impending anxiousness of war about to break out in the Mid-East. Jesus said, *"My people, I sense a disturbance and stress among the factions in Israel. There can be no peace among threats and terrorists. There is no room for love in their hearts when their minds are full of hate for each other. I tell you again, to pray for peace in your world that is teetering toward war. Man has too much pride to live in peace, because it will mean giving something up in compromise. But unless some are willing to accommodate compromise, there will be a severe confrontation. Know that the evil one will have his hand in bringing discord at this time. Satan's time is about to come to an end and he will be unleashing all of his fury against man, shortly. Look to the seeds of this last Battle of Armageddon. The time of the Antichrist's declaration is not far off. You must come to Me in love to seek protection from all of these hateful factions. The power struggles between good and evil are about to clash."*

Later, at the prayer group, I could see a mother home schooling her children. Jesus said, *"My dear parents, remember you are responsible for bringing the knowledge of faith to your children and grandchildren. For those that go to the trouble of teaching their children at home, a special grace will go out to your family. In many places, the home may be the only place that your children may receive the proper training. Those considering this choice may need to seek help from others. In your days of the Apostasy, this may soon be your only choice."*

I could see some children in a dark room not getting the proper attention to their needs. Jesus said, *"My people, be careful where you leave your children. Some children may be abused in various places of day-care. Even accredited schools may still receive the wrong influence from teachers who are not training with a proper moral code. It is again your responsibility to check on what your children are being taught. Many are receiving too worldly an environment to keep close to Me."*

I could see some cigarettes and a tray of sweet foods. Jesus said, *"My people, you must be aware of your bad habits that can lead you to a more worldly life. You have many comforts and many fine foods. Do not become so influenced that you appease all of your appetites in an unbridled manner. Protect your body from excesses and train your self-control with fasting. Be willing to suffer for My Name's sake all that you are tested with. See with My help that your trials will seem easy to suffer as a prayer to Me."*

I could see a house with a large front window. Jesus said, *"My people, I call your attention to how you appear to those around you. You profess to be one of My faithful. Do others, that see you every day, recognize you as one of My servants? You must be careful by your example in how you lead your life. In everything you do, your actions speak louder than your words. So be conscious of giving good example to your neighbor. If you are to lead souls to Me, you must practice every day that which you are preaching. Show others by your frequent prayer and going to Confession that you do seek to be My disciple."*

I could see a farm silo and then the scene turned into turrets on a castle. Jesus said, *"My people, you must be ever on guard to protect your family from the snares of Satan. By blessing your home and praying together as a family, you can guide all of your family members and protect their souls. Provide for their needs during the coming tribulation with your food stock. Keep your holy statues, icons, and crucifixes in the home to give signs of Our Presence. This is why many signs of faith support are being given in changing Rosaries, weeping statues and icons."*

I could see a woman with an unusual amount of make-up on and then I saw Mary's face with her radiant natural appearance. Mary said, *"My dear sisters, your Lord provided you with a beautiful face and body. Do not be so concerned to alter your appearance with artificial means. Learn to accept what the Lord has given you and not to cover yourself up with an unnatural appearance. Give glory to God that you are pleasing enough in His sight, just as you were created. Follow my example in living to be humble in the Lord's service. This is all that is required and not to be someone that you are not."*

I could see transmitters of radio and TV and then some receiving dishes to receive those signals. Jesus said, *"My people, many of My children are living their lives so they can spend their time with constant entertainment. There is more to life than movies, TV and radio. Do not let these things control you. If you spend all of your free time with such occupation, how will you have time for Me in prayer, or time for seeing many other experiences in life. You can spend your time helping others as well, so you are not selfish with your time and talents. So go and live a proper Christian life of service to God and neighbor, and be unfettered by so many distractions of the world."*

Friday, August 8, 1997:

After Communion, I could see a large host emanating light and it was among some very dark clouds. Jesus said, *"My people, My love for you knows no bounds. You must see in this vision how I will lead all of My people during the coming purification. I am showing you My Host, because I will enable My angels to bring My Heavenly Manna to you during the tribulation. My faithful remnant will be underground for a brief trial, but then you will soon share in My Triumph. Do not let your souls be downcast, but lift up your hearts to see My miraculous intervention in your history. Do not fear any of these trials, but place your full trust in My protection from evil. Pray for strength in this time and I will guide you as I did My people of Israel in ancient times. I am the same God ever present, guarding My flock. Have confidence in Me and you will soon be rewarded for your faithfulness in My new Era of Peace."*

Later, at Adoration, I could look down and see a circle of men wearing different uniforms of various countries. Jesus said, *"My people, you are seeing the many troops that make up the police force for the United Nations. Many nations contribute troops for peace keeping around the world. These troops will become innocent helpers that will be abused by the Antichrist. These well-meaning people will get taken up by the charisma and suggestion of the Antichrist in the name of peace. He will gradually win their hearts over to help him save the world from a coming food crisis and the chaos that will go with it. He will station troops all over the world to control the borders and allow him to ration the scarce food supplies. He will subtly bring the mark of the beast to buy and sell and soon many will come to worship the Antichrist and thank him for supplying the food. He will reach to control the whole world through the United Nations forces. Just as he thinks that he has won over mankind, I will smite him, his followers and the demons. With My Triumph none of these will ever walk the Earth again, for I will condemn this lot to Hell. But My remnant I will lift up in the glory of My Era of Peace. Pray, My children, that all of your trials and anxieties will all be put to rest in My love. Come to Me now, so you can prepare to endure this brief purification."*

Saturday, August 9, 1997:

After Communion, I could see a path down a dark stony road hemmed in by old houses. Jesus said, *"My people, I come to you each day to ask you to follow in My footsteps. You have heard the expression of walking a mile in My sandals. Now, I beg you to take up your daily cross and carry it for the sake of My love. I give you many gifts in this world. This is the one favor that I ask in return, that you follow My Will even in suffering. I had to suffer and die for all of your sins. See that whatever struggles you must go through each day, you offer up to Me so you may gain the merits of that suffering in the after life. These heavenly merits will be stored up in Heaven to weigh against all of your sins at the judgment time. When I call you home, you will be remembered as I beckon you to come and enjoy the banquet of your master. Prepare in your suffering now, and your eternal life with me will be assured. This invitation of Mine, to come to the wedding feast, is not to be taken lightly nor are you to be late in coming to it."*

Later, at the Church of the Nativity, St. Paul, Minnesota, after Communion, I could see some pipes of an organ and they were arrayed as trumpets. Jesus said, *"My people, soon My angels will sound the trumpets of the Last Days. At that time, all that has been foretold in the Scriptures will come to pass. Even though these days may seem fearsome, rest in your spirit that I will deliver My faithful through your trials. Just as man has used his weapons to make war, I will beat these weapons into things of peace to make all men aware of My love. You will live to see My day when all the evil before you will be wiped away. Have faith and trust in Me that whatever has been foretold by My Word, will be fulfilled. Heaven is announcing for you to prepare at this time, for all of these events are about to take place."*

Sunday, August 10, 1997:

At St. Pius X Church, Zimmerman, Minnesota, after Communion, I could see someone had packed some bags for travel. Jesus said, *"My people, you are masters of preparation when you choose to travel. You plan for months where you will go, taking care to get plane tickets in advance. You may even buy special clothes and plan your itinerary to the last detail. I mention this in contrast to the most important trip of your life. That is when you travel to your eternal destination after death. Your plans should be made for this journey with even more care than your earthly trips. Your tickets to Heaven involve a lifetime commitment of following My Will. Your dress will be the grace of all the sacraments, especially at Confession where you are forgiven your sins and made radiant in My sight. With such plans in place, you will see that there is only one joy in the assurance of My love in bringing you to Heaven. It is this everlasting peace and love with Me that burns in all of your souls. So go, and throughout your lives be ever ready for this, your most important trip."*

Later, at the Epiphany Church, Coon Rapids, Minnesota, before the Blessed Sacrament, I could see a white streak of light bend in an arc from left to right. Jesus said, *"My people, I am showing you the comet of the great chastisement. It is already directed toward Earth and it will not be changed from its orbit. It will not be long and you will hear of its discovery. At first it will be kept secret so as not to raise fear among the people. The information will be leaked out as the military will try to destroy it. I have shown you before that My angels will deflect any attempts to destroy it. Do not be fearful, My children, but be in preparation. Those in the caves would be most protected. This is the instrument that I will use to thwart Satan of his brief reign. Continue to prepare spiritually, for you know not the time I will call you home to Me."*

Monday, August 11, 1997:

After Communion, I could see an empty plate set for supper. Jesus said, *"My people, you always have assumed that there will be enough food to place on your plate each supper. Yet, there are many people around the world who are not as fortunate to expect this. Soon many will suffer from this food shortage for many reasons. Getting food to various suppliers will soon become a difficult task. Other forces will take advantage of this problem to have control over the people. You, My friends, do not have to worry. I have asked you to be prepared for this coming shortage. I will even multiply what you have for your survival and you will have no need to depend on others. The Antichrist will exploit this situation for his own gain, but he will be thwarted after a short reign."*

Later, I could see three dolls, but there was something evil about them. Jesus said, *"My people, your children are pure and innocent at the outset. In your fast-paced society, you are too anxious to leave your children with others to be cared for. It is more important, where possible, to take a lesser standard of living so the mother can care for her young children. It is also important to know what your children are being taught. Give them each the deposit of faith that all of them need to come and know Me. It is your responsibility to lead their souls on the right path to Heaven. If life is troublesome because of the children's environment, do whatever is necessary in prayer to provide the proper Christian environment. Once you have provided the proper training, you can be satisfied that you did My Will. It will then be the child's free will to accept Me on their own. Pray for your children and do everything in your power to keep these souls close to Me."*

Tuesday, August 12, 1997:

After Communion, I could see a brochure for traveling to some islands. Jesus said, *"My people, it is not necessary to travel abroad in order to satisfy your earthly desires for pleasure. Many feel that unless they can travel overseas, they have not experienced life. There is nothing new under the sun overseas than what is in your place as well. Do not aspire to such dreams of new places when they are not necessary. Many times you build up your hopes in anticipation of great things, but once you realize your dream location, it is not so rewarding. Desires of earthly things will always leave you empty and cold because you are drawn more to spiritual goals to be satisfied. It is only when your souls come to Me that your joy will know no end. The things of this life pass away tomorrow, but the spiritual things last forever. So, seek the heavenly treasures instead of those on Earth, and your soul will find its true goal."*

Later, at Adoration, I could see some heavily armed black helicopters in the sky. Jesus said, *"My people, Satan and his agents have been building their organizations for years. It is only in recent years that technology has allowed these evil men to put in place a secret organization that could dominate the whole world. These evil men and the demons are allowed to go only so far. They know I hold the ultimate power against them and that they have only a short time left. So do not be fearful of these men and their weapons. I can force their weapons to be useless at any time. Always dwell on the fact that I am the victor over evil and I only am testing you. By My purification, I will remove all evil from the world. These evil men may think that they are in control, but their insignificant power will not even last but a moment. Against Me and My angels, their fate is sealed. So concentrate, My friends, on your spiritual duty to save souls. That is enough for your concern. I will deal with these evil forces when they are all cast into Hell. Pray for these lost souls that they may come to the light, before it is too late."*

Wednesday, August 13, 1997:

After Communion, I could see a monstrance with the Host and rays of light beaming out from it. The Host became the pupil of the eye of God. Jesus said, *"My people, I am forever present among you, but in an even more special way in My Eucharist. This Real Presence you know and adore, I have given witness to in many miracles of My Eucharist. For those of you who have not heard of My Hosts bleeding or turning into My Real Flesh, you need to search for this information. These miracles, when understood, give proof to even the unbelievers of My True Presence in the Host. For those who fail to believe in My Real Presence, I will bring you My grace of understanding, if your spirit is open. For those who refuse to believe in My Real Presence, even faced with this witness, then there is some question of your understanding of why I died for you. Read the Scriptures and you will learn to know Me. You must truly accept Me into the love of your hearts. Otherwise, you are only going through the motions."*

Thursday, August 14, 1997: (Maximilian Kolbe)

After Communion, I could see a series of tall mountains and then I was looking into a drop hole for a gallows. Jesus said, *"My people, you are all prisoners of this life and doomed to a life of suffering. You are to follow in My footsteps to the Cross on Calvary. Do not look to this world for joy and pleasure, for this is a vale of tears. By Adam's sin you are condemned to a life vulnerable to grief and you have to work for your sustenance. Very few things in this life are easy and most require suffering to survive. Each day you have to sweat by your brow to exist. If I did not come and give up My life that you may have eternal life, your future would have been hopeless. So see that My Redemption has loosed your bonds of sin, and you have a new life in My Holy Spirit. Rejoice, My children, even though you may have to suffer now, My faithful will enjoy the fruits of their labor in My Name. No matter how much you suffer now, you have been promised to be with Me in the glory of Heaven. You all have been given the sentence to die once. It is only a matter of time until that day I call you to judgment. So, My friends, if you suffer and struggle for the sake of Me and your neighbor, it will not be in vain, but a labor of love. Look to this world as a means of salvation, so you will be tested and found to be true to My Word. When all is done, you will follow My outstretched arms as I lead you home to your eternal home with Me."*

At the prayer group, I could see a wide panorama of an atomic explosion going off. Mary came and said, *"My dear children, this is why I wanted you to commit yourself to my heavenly consecration. Once you are united with me and my Son, you will be focused to pray my three Rosaries each day for peace in the world.*

Pray in earnest, my dear children, for a nuclear war hangs in the balance. With so many nations in possession of atomic weapons, there can be a multitude of possibilities to trigger such a disaster. Pray that men's hearts will be opened, so peace may reign over the Earth instead of war."

I could see an older man and there were dropclothes covering some large statues to protect them. Jesus said, *"My people, it will not be long until they will start closing the churches. You may be called on to preserve these statues that will be hard to replace. My mother's statue is visiting your area now, and she draws all her faithful to her. Seek out My daily Mass as often as you can attend, for you know not how much longer you will have this treasure available."*

I could see some large crowds flocking to a church. Jesus said, *"My people, as it becomes apparent about the Antichrist's coming, there will be an increased holiness given to My faithful. Evil will also strengthen in various ways. There will be a large division between all the good and all the evil. This battle of good and evil will be accentuated right up until the Battle of Armageddon."*

I could see a picture of the prayer card with God the Father over Jesus on the Cross. God the Father came and said, *"I Am has heard your dedication of your prayer group to My honor. I treasure your wife's inspiration in My heart. It is not long ago when you witnessed to My Son's Transfiguration when I asked you to listen to Him. Whenever you call on Me in the Our Father, I am present watching over you. Follow My Son's Will and you will be following My Will as well. If I may impose on you, recite a special prayer to Me at the beginning of your prayer service, so all may know of your acknowledging Me."*

I could see a setting sun reflect off a huge boat which looked like that of Noah's Ark. Jesus said, *"My people, as you view the rainbow, you are reminded of My Covenant with you in not flooding the world again. This vision I am showing you because the evil of your day is crying out for vengeance, in answer to the justice given at the time of Noah. I will always protect My faithful, even if I visit the Earth with destruction. Know that this age's days are numbered, for My great chastisement is being readied.*

See, My people, to prepare yourself for judgment. The day of My Triumph will be upon you soon. Take care to ready yourself with Confession to purify all your souls."

I could see some men fighting verbally and shouting at each other. Jesus said, *"My friends, you must stop your bickering with each other over earthly things. Change your hearts over from one of hatred to one of love. If you do not change your ways, your hate will consume you. Satan is challenging you every day to cause dissension over anything your pride will allow. Pray to deny him of these opportunities to spread division. It is much easier to destroy than to build friendships. Making true friends takes care and understanding. How valuable a true friend can be even amidst adversity."*

I could see a long procession carrying a casket to rest in a dark stony tomb. Jesus said, *"My people, it is proper to come and grieve together with another's lost loved one. Be gracious in giving of your time to share with those in need of your consolation. I am the Resurrection and the Life. Bring all of these dying souls before Me so they may be made ready for their coming to rest with Me in Heaven. Give prayers and service to all in need of your help."*

Friday, August 15, 1997: (Assumption)

After Communion, I could see Our Lady's beautiful face and she was dressed in blue and white. Mary said, *"My dear children, I come dressed in the sun to give witness to this glorification of my place in Heaven. I was called blessed because of my Lord's calling to be His mother. It is this celebration of my being assumed into Heaven that gives you faith in being resurrected one day. All of the souls on Earth are called to be with God. It is not your destiny to remain on earth, but to be forever with your Lord. So lift up your hearts and follow my Son, Jesus' Will for you. It is only by accepting His call and giving Him your 'yes' that you will be taken up to Heaven. Those who refuse to accept Him as Master of their lives, will have to accept eternal torture from the demons in their place in Hell. Come to my Son now and you will never suffer any pain again. The love of my Son is all that drove me through life. See that His love calls you to Him. He is the eternal desire of all souls. Do not hesitate, but come to adore Him forever."*

Later, during a Spiritual Communion, I could see a picture of Muriel's mother and she said, *"Thank you for taking the time to listen for me. I love my daughter, Muriel, and all of my family for the help they gave me. I was waiting to hear David's voice before I wanted to leave. I am in a heavenly place with no more pain. My husband greeted me as I arrived. Do not worry about me and I will be praying for all of you full-time."*

Saturday, August 16, 1997:

At the Cathedral in Santa Fe, New Mexico, after Communion, I could see some Franciscans dressed in brown greeting me and showing me through an historical church. Jesus said, *"My friends, this is a place of deep faith. Many years ago missionaries brought the faith to this area. Because of the dedication and devotion of the people here, I have blessed this area very much with My presence. While some visit the landmarks, the real treasure here is My deposit of faith. Wherever you find Me in My Sacrament of the Eucharist, you have My Real Presence. My graces and blessings need to be shared with your neighbors. My love cannot be contained, so go out into all the nations and spread My Words of love that all mankind may know Me. It is beautiful to give witness to My name and My love. The more you spread My Word, the more you will be blessed in your work of evangelization. Continue to follow My Will in all I ask of you. Give thanks to God that you have this time to praise and adore your God."*

Later, at the Blessed Sacrament Chapel in Espanola, New Mexico, I could see Jesus and He was walking among all the hills and mountains around us. Jesus said, *"My people, look all around you and see the true beauty of My Creation. Many times you take pride in your work, but look how small man's things are compared to the panorama around you. Do not dwell on your pride, but give thanks to Me for My gifts in all that you have and do. Give thanks to Me for all that you accomplish, for without My help, you could do nothing. When you think more of crediting your Lord, you will spend less time on your foolish pride. Be focused on doing everything for Me, and you will receive blessings beyond your dreams."*

Sunday, August 17, 1997:

At the Community Center Church, Albuquerque, New Mexico, after Communion, I could see a dark cloudy sky and there was a strong wind. Then the clouds parted and a gleaming Host with a bright light came down from Heaven. Jesus said, *"My people, every time you come to share in the Sacrifice of the Mass, I give you My Body to eat and My Blood to drink. When you receive Me in Holy Communion, you are joined in My One Spirit and My One Body. You are flesh and spirit, and with your holy reception of Me, your flesh and spirit becomes united with Mine. See, My children, that I offer Myself to you everyday that you can receive Me. I am your Daily Bread, come down from Heaven, so your spirit may be fed My heavenly blessings. Even during the tribulation, I will make Myself available to you. If you cannot have the Mass, seek Me in Spiritual Communion and My angels will deliver My Sacred Body to your lips. I will feed you My Heavenly Manna as I fed the multitude in the desert. Have faith and full trust that I will always feed you, so your spirit may always enjoy My love and peace. Come to Me, My children, and My protection will always surround your soul. My faithful should never fear the evil one, for I will always be there watching over you."*

Monday, August 18, 1997:

After Communion, I could see a Communion rail with people kneeling. Jesus said, *"My people, I am grateful to all who give Me reverence in My Blessed Sacrament. It is important to remember to give honor and praise to Me and not just the traditions. You have seen the Scribes and Pharisees follow the law of traditions, even when their hearts were far from Me. Do not force others to follow these traditions unless they are really doing it from their hearts. It is your humble submission to My Will that I am seeking, not just to follow traditions. Still, there are cases where there have been irreverences in your churches as well. You should give My Blessed Sacrament proper respect by having it in a place of honor in My church. When you come to church, you come to respect Me, not just the altar. Those that belittle Confession and prayer are doing My people more of a disservice. It is important to seek My forgiveness of your sins at all times. Those who do not*

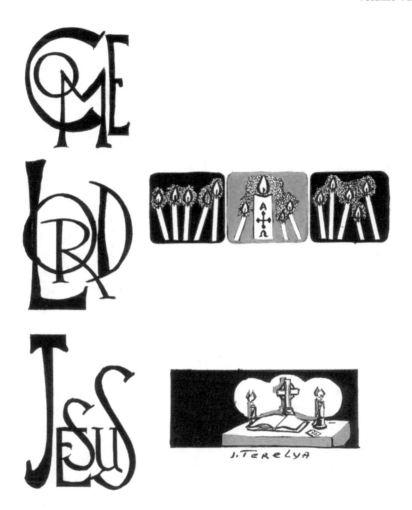

COME LORD JESUS

J. TERELYA

speak of sin and the forgiveness of sin are avoiding their duty to save souls. See that bringing souls to Me is the most significant thing you can do while you are on the Earth. It is this battle to save souls that is what life is all about. So come to Me, My children, to seek salvation for yourself and your neighbor."

Later, at Adoration, I could see two candles burning on an altar with a dim light. I then saw many people sitting at different tables and they all had two lit candles on their tables. Jesus said, *"My people, I am the eternal light always burning brightly in your life. At the Mass these two candles give light and praise to My most beautiful gift to humanity—the Mass. To keep My Light burning in your heart, I offer you My Real Presence to receive under the appearances of bread and wine. Whenever you have the opportunity to come to Mass, you are blessed to receive Me in this sacred union of our spirits. When you see the two candles at each table, I am showing you how each of you can receive Me into your house and your own hearts. I have told you that I would be present with you to the end of time. Just call on Me at any time and I will be there with you to help in your needs. More importantly, think to give Me praise and thanks for all the many blessings that I bestow on each of you. Your Communion is a thanksgiving by its own meaning. So keep Me close in your thoughts throughout the whole day. I am with you every moment of every day, so do not hesitate to acknowledge My Presence. Hold Me close to your heart until the day I can welcome you into your home with Me in Heaven."*

Tuesday, August 19, 1997:

After Communion, I could see some rocks and stone figures. Jesus said, *"My people, I am showing you these rocks because you must be strong in the faith. I called St. Peter a rock because I wanted My Church to be solidly founded. You must be deeply rooted in your faith with a sound foundation in My Commandments. You are led in My Church by My vicar in Pope John Paul II, who gives you direction while you cannot see Me physically. My pope son is a sign to you of the authority I have given to My Church. Listen to him when he speaks of faith and morals. The Holy Spirit operates through him to lead My faithful. Much like Gideon, who sought a sign of the angel's words, I have given you many signs to strengthen your faith and witness to My Presence among you."* Note: Recently, Adrian Sanchez shared a special gift with us on his recent conversion. He was struggling to convert and the Lord gave him a miraculous sign on his shovel from work. On the shovel was a very obvious picture of Jesus' face as on the Shroud of Turin.

Later, at Adoration, I could see a daylight scene of many people going up a hill. Once on the hill, everyone could see the white cross of the permanent sign. Those looking upon it were healed of

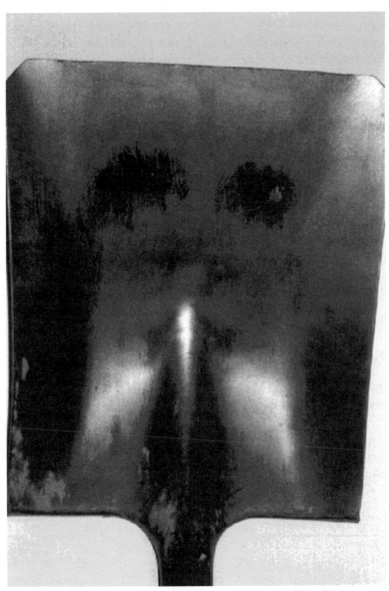

Face of Jesus on Adrian Sanchez's shovel.

any sickness. Jesus said, *"My people, see how wondrous is your God. In your time of need during the tribulation, I will perform many miracles through My angels. When you are led to My refuges of protection, you will be in awe of My power. Just as I protected the Israelites from Pharaoh's army, I will protect you from the Antichrist and the demons. See how many will be cared for in all of their physical and spiritual needs. Those fortunate to be under My protection, will marvel at My wondrous sign of love. Even so, there will be many who will be persecuted for My Name's sake. Some will die as martyrs at the hands of these treacherous evil men at that time. Those martyred will live in my Era of Peace. You may have to suffer for a moment, but you will be joyful at your reward. No matter what you may face in this tribulation, have trust that I will be guarding your souls. All of Scripture must be fulfilled, so prepare, My children, to receive the purification of this evil age."*

Wednesday, August 20, 1997:

After Communion, I could see my hands in prayer and a white flash of light beside me. Jesus said, *"My people, many find this reading of the owner of the vineyard hard to understand. I hold out hope to the sinner, that even in the last hour, I will allow them to be saved. Many of the rich will find the poor walking into Heaven ahead of them, since the rich had less to suffer on Earth than the poor. Again, some, who are new converts, may go before you, who have been with Me a long time. They were placed ahead of you because they had to suffer more and struggled to be saved, despite odds against them. Your earthly justice pales before My heavenly mercy and love. I look into the hearts and I judge according to My ways, instead of your ways. So do not make judgments on your fellow men, since I treat all of you equally in allowing everyone to come to Heaven. If I should choose to save those that were lost, rejoice that My mercy goes far beyond your judgment. It is enough for each of you to find your way to salvation. So do not worry why I choose some to be saved that seem unworthy to you. Instead, rejoice that I will accept sinners even at the eleventh hour."*

Thursday, August 21, 1997: (St. Pius X)

After Communion, I could see a large, late model car sitting in a green field. Jesus said, *"My people, on the day I called My Apostles to follow Me, I did not ask them to bring all of their possessions, but to walk in faith. Even when I sent My Apostles out to preach to all nations, again I told them to take nothing extra. The laborer for souls is worth his wage of the kindness of those he visits. So it is with you, as you approach the tribulation. You are to go into hiding with only what you can carry. Be prepared most for your spiritual attacks with many sacramentals. Take your Rosaries, Crucifixes, Holy Water, Bibles, and blessed candles. Be prepared to leave your houses and cars behind. The more you trust in Me, I will provide for your physical and spiritual needs. It is this full trust in My protection that will guard you. If you do all of this for My Name's sake to avoid the evil one, your reward will be seen in My Era of Peace."*

Later, at the prayer group I could see many people coming together in the open at a refuge site. Jesus said, *"My people, you will be rejoicing to join Me with your angels at My places of refuge. All of My faithful will find great consolation in trusting in My help for them. Many may have fear of what will come, but ask My help and a great peace will come over your soul. When you see Me come among you with My heavenly bread, you will praise Me in My glory as the people of the Exodus believed in Me."*

I could see a house that was insulated and the walls were not finished. It was in an attic of a house used for hiding. Jesus said, *"My people, in many miraculous ways, I will lead you to safe havens on your way to your final destination of hiding. I will help you find places of protection along the way when you need help with food or lodging. Many now are inspired to make places of refuge in helping those persecuted. Those, who give this help, will find a heavenly reward awaiting them."*

I could see a huge crevasse from an earthquake where the two plates were pulling away from each other. Jesus said, *"My people, you will see great changes made on the Earth's surface as huge earthquakes and volcanoes will reshape the dry land. There will be much death and suffering when these great disturbances will occur. There will be nothing that you can do because these things will take place swiftly with no warning. Be ever prepared spiritually, because you know not when you will be called home to judgment. So continue your frequent fervent confessions so your souls are always ready to receive Me."*

I could see many warplanes preparing for some strikes and there were large plumes of bombs going off. Jesus said, *"My people, you will see a new war that will draw many nations in a confrontation. Satan will be instigating more wars with wider involvement than some of your smaller wars. As the wars approach the time of the Antichrist, they will gain in intensity of battle. Soon these battles will be between the faithful and the unbelievers."*

I could see a huge blue globe with the sun coming as rays all around the globe. In the middle of the globe I could see the Two Hearts of Jesus and Mary. Mary said, *"My dear children, I came as a woman dressed in the sun to share our Two Hearts of love with your heart. We come in triumph, my children, so do not have any fear of what is to come. We have suffered before you, as you must suffer during this tribulation. You will see your suffering will be one of joy, because you will be protected by my mantle. Stay close to the both of Us and We will guide you on your way."*

I could see some white crosses, but then I was shown some other crosses with the corpus on them. Jesus said, *"My people, be careful to test the spirit of all miraculous signs that will be given. Satan will try to imitate My crosses in having them strangely appear. Test the fruits of the spirit at these places. Trust more in Crucifixes that have My Corpus on them. The evil one cannot witness to My Suffering on the Cross. When you hold up My Crucifix, it will reveal to you if a miracle is from Me or Satan."*

I could see the Earth as a globe in space and I could view a comet coming toward the Earth. As the comet approached the Earth, it became so bright that it appeared as if there were two suns. Jesus said, *"My people, this fiery chastisement is coming as a great cataclysm about to collide with the Earth. It is during the coming of this comet in all of its fury that it may convince some souls to make a last minute conversion. Do not wait until the last moment of this judgment. You need to make ready to receive Me even now. The more you put off your conversion, the larger the chance that you may be condemned to Hell. Convert now while you still have time to allow Me to run your lives."*

Friday, August 22, 1997: (Queenship of Mary)

After Communion, I could see a large thick spider web. Jesus said, *"My people, beware of the evil one who is always lurking to snare souls in his traps of worldly things. Do not be so easily seduced by something new. All of your dependencies on worldly distractions take you further away from Me. Keep My pictures, statues and Rosaries about you, so you can keep Me ever in your thoughts. The day that you leave Me out of your sight could be the day Satan will enter your heart. Be always on the lookout for how the evil one will trip you up with temptations. Desire only to follow My Will and you will forever be guarded against evil. The more you know of his workings in these snares, the more you will know what to avoid. Do not seek fame or riches in this life, or your pride will consume you. Seek to please Me only and you will find focusing on Me will lead you away from sin."*

Later, after Communion, I could see Jesus on the Cross. Next to Him was Mary and behind her was a beautiful gold curtain. Mary came and said, *"My dear child, I am happy you saw the light to come visit my Statue of Fatima. Sometimes you have to set aside your own desires, so you can be open to the Spirit of God. This is a beautiful feast and a joyous time for all of you to share in my consecration. It is my Son, Jesus, who has glorified me. He is the one who has called me blessed before all of mankind. He is the one who assumed me into Heaven. It is by His grace alone that I have been made Queen of Heaven. Our hearts are one and I give praise and glory to my Son. I am the one who leads you to my Son. When you see me, you know my Son, Jesus, is close by. Rejoice, my children, and give honor to my Queenship, but remain humble in your faith, for you know not when temptation will come against you. By always uniting yourself with our Two Hearts, you continue to keep focused on your Lord. Be thankful that you have such a loving Lord in all He does for you."*

Saturday, August 23, 1997:

After Communion, I could see some empty seats in a church. This was followed by seeing a pair of eyes with darkness all about them. Jesus said, *"My people, I am showing you many weak souls who know they should be coming to give Me worship, but they are too lazy in spirit to move themselves to come. Satan has grabbed hold of their hearts for their desires of sin and the things of this world. Even though many were given the faith and know better, they are too much in love with their sins to come to Me. It is this group of fallen away faithful that you need to pray for and encourage back to the Church. Without Me, a soul will be lost. That is why it is important to convert these souls, since they could be lost forever if no one helps them. My faithful are responsible to go out and save souls that should be with Me. Do not give up on these souls, but especially be patient and seek to bring them back to Me. Heaven rejoices over the least significant soul that chooses to return from being lost. You, My friends, can be the instrument of their salvation. Reach out and do your duty. If you have tried, and they still refuse over time, then they alone will be responsible for their loss."*

Later, at Adoration, I could see a pair of glasses in the distance. I came closer to look through the glasses and everything became clearer. Jesus said, *"My people, I am asking you to put on your spiritual glasses, so you can understand what is going on around you. When you have prayer in your heart and you look through the eyes of faith, you will see more purpose in your life in following My Will. When you look through the eyes of My suffering, you can look out and see how much My people have to suffer as I did and as I still suffer. Living in pain makes you humble, yet at the same time, you can offer up your pain for a good prayer petition. When you suffer for My Name's sake, you may have to suffer criticism and other discomforts of the body. Hold all of the body's desires for creature comforts in check, and be willing to suffer for Me any indignation that will challenge you. You know that you have to do some suffering to gain your salvation. So do not reject suffering, but see it as a means to strive for My Heavenly Kingdom. You will be tested, but always look to My help to get you through."*

Sunday, August 24, 1997:

After Communion, I could see a big fish underwater in a stream. Jesus said, *"My people, I am calling on all of My evangelists at this time to be fishers of men, as I called My Apostles to preach to all the nations. What you are seeing are the poor souls immersed in their sin, whom you must go and catch to bring them to My Kingdom. The harvest of souls is great, but there are few willing to go out into the byroads to deliver My message of saving their souls. All of those souls being converted and brought to Me now, have been given a great privilege of grace in this evil age. See the urgency in My request to save as many souls as possible at this time, because soon the time for conversion will be lost. Woe is that person in the time of My coming judgment who has not yet accepted Me as their Savior. Those who refuse Me or are luke-warm without any roots, will be cast into the fiery furnace of Hell forever. Wake up, My people, and come to your Master who awaits to lift all of your burdens. Suffer for Me now, or you will suffer even more in vain for those who will be lost."*

Later, at Adoration, I could see two men fighting with swords and shields. Jesus said, *"My people, man has been fighting throughout history, but this fighting in the future will be for survival. As the famine and pestilence comes to the world, many will be fighting for goods and food. There will be a massive world depression that will cause national economic systems to falter and some to fail. Many will become so desperate for help to quell the riots and food shortages, that they will accept the man of peace in the Antichrist. He will be allowed to control everyone by their buying and selling with the chip. Many of My faithful will reject him and his so-called help. I will at that time provide for you, My children. Do not fear what you will eat or drink or the power of the evil one. You may suffer discomfort for a while, but your faith in Me will bring you an eternal reward. Do not complain as the Israelites did in the desert, but just have patience for a short time and your hearts will have everything you could ever desire. Your faith and trust in Me will save you from any danger."*

Monday, August 25, 1997:

After Communion, I could see a heart shape and it became imbedded in a large building. It kept going deeper into the building to become a part of it. Jesus said, *"My people, you must take My love and make it a part of all of your society. My love should be a part of the mortar that binds you all together. Faith and belief in My laws should be the basic building blocks of all that you do. See how pervasive is My love, that all creation is focused around it. Many times you may love one another and not always appreciate how much I pour My love out on each and everyone of My creatures. Think of how intimate you are with all of My creation. My love is wrapped around you even more so. I ask you to reach out and love Me, so your soul can taste a little of My infinite love for you. See how I gave up My life for you, because I love you so much and I wanted your sins forgiven. If you love Me, seek forgiveness of your sins in Confession. With a clean soul, you will be radiant with My love in you."*

Later, at Adoration, I could see many flames as a church was being burned up. Then I saw the caves of protection like the catacombs. Jesus said, *"My people, many of My churches will be destroyed or abandoned as the Antichrist will persecute My Church. My faithful remnant will be split from the side of the Church that refuses to follow My traditions and the Ten Commandments. This schism in My Church will drive My faithful to an underground Church. Those in control of the schismatic church will mislead even some of My elect. To avoid the powers of the Antichrist and his desire to kill My faithful, you will have to seek hiding in caves as in previous persecutions. Do not fear this time, for My grace of protection will go forward in the help of My angels. You will witness a great battle for souls. Reach out now to establish your prayer groups, where you will find My strength. It is important to convert souls before it may be too late. Once the Antichrist establishes his reign, you will only survive spiritually through My help. Those that refuse to seek My help at that time, will surely be lost."*

Tuesday, August 26, 1997:

After Communion, I could see a grotto to the Blessed Virgin Mary in the rock and there was a spring of water coming out. Mary came and said, *"My dear children, at several places that I have appeared to my children, Heaven has granted a miraculous spring of water to give witness of the truth. You are all seeking signs to confirm that which is obvious. Because of your weak faith, many signs have been given even in such waters that are miraculous for healing. Still many have not believed in me nor my Son, even with evidence of heavenly intervention. There are still a lot of uncaring souls that do not want to listen to the messages from Heaven. It is not a question if these signs are real, but many souls are refusing my Son as master over their lives. The giving up of their will to the Divine Will is the hard condition for being saved. So do not seek signs in themselves, but seek to give your heart and soul over to the service of your Lord. In the end, it is this giving over of your will that Jesus needs to bring you home to Heaven."*

Later, at Adoration, I could see some Zodiac signs written across a street with chalk. Jesus said, *"My people, do not follow the witchcraft of fortune tellers or the horoscopes of the astrologers. In your human weakness, you sometimes seek the fancy of knowing the future. Do not concern yourself with what will happen tomorrow. Today has enough troubles of its own. It is not necessary to know if you will be rich or live a long life. It is only important to follow My Will for you, which is to lead a good Christian life. If you spent more time thinking how to imitate Me, instead of following your own fantasies, you would gain more in your spiritual life. Do not follow your every desire, but control your will in giving yourself over to Me. By living your consecration to Me and My mother, you will be fully focused on your spiritual future, instead of seeking after only your earthly future."*

Wednesday, August 27, 1997:

After Communion, I could see a woman who seemed to be in deep stress. Jesus said, *"My people, many women in today's world have had to suffer from bad marriages. Either abuse or infidelity has caused many divorces. This is a difficult area where Church law deals with the annulment process. Where someone's physical or spiritual life is threatened, there is a grave concern. In some of these cases, it is better for a separation. It is unfortunate that personal desires are pursued over love of the spouse or over abiding by the marriage contract. My faithful couples should show each other their love in ways to keep their marriage consecrated to Me. I am in the middle of all marriages through the sacramental bond. Be committed to each other and be willing to care for each other. Fighting is no way to love each other, so avoid things that would cause arguments. In all marriages, you should strive to love as I love My Church. Let your life and vocation in marriage be your means of salvation for each other. Look forward to saving marriages rather than for the least little excuse to end a marriage."*

Thursday, August 28, 1997:

After Communion, I could see a car and a large wave of water inundating the car. There was a dark and stormy scene at night. Jesus said, *"My people, soon you will see some massive destruction from a huge storm. Water will cause a major flood for a brief time. You have seen such storms before, but the intensity of these storms will cause some fears. Your country will continue to suffer these chastisements because you have failed to listen to My warnings. Your sins are so heaped on each other and you have not even feared My judgments. The punishment for your abortions and sins of the flesh is being called down on you. I have mercy on sinners, but your complacency and open defiance of My laws are calling My justice against you. Prepare to be tested, for these things will come upon you very suddenly. Awaken from your sins, America. Come to Me seeking forgiveness and these things can be mitigated. Without prayer and forgiveness, you can expect the worst."*

Later, at the prayer group, I could see an old picture with a Host held over the Cup. Jesus said, *"My people, you are to do everything in your power to continue respect for My Real Presence in the bread and wine. Even though some may not believe in My Real Presence, I am still there. The more you can promote Perpetual Adoration, the more blessings will be on your parish. Those who adore Me and give Me time out of their busy schedules, will be rewarded in the hereafter."*

I could see a carnival with many noises and lights. Jesus said, *"My people, do not be so taken up with your entertainment, that you forget to give Me time in prayer. The more you pray and flee away from this world's distractions, the more your spiritual life will be allowed to grow. Remember that you are the one limiting our love relationship. The more you love Me, the more you will want to spend prayer time with Me. Come at any time and I will be happy to receive you."*

I could see some evil leaders and their faces were covered with a black shroud. Jesus said, *"My people, these evil leaders will be leading the world into some serious conflicts that could take many lives. I repeat My mother's request for prayers for peace in your world."*

I could see some people helping to bring the Pilgrim Statue of Fatima around to the churches here in Rochester. Mary came and said, *"My dear children, I wish to give a special thank you to all of my children who came forward to honor my Statue of Fatima. It is the workers who made this trip possible, that I especially want to thank. By keeping my image before you, you can see how I am intercessor for your prayers to be given to my Son, Jesus. All Heaven rejoices always, when my children gather in prayer around me."*

I could see in the desert where Our Blessed Lord retreated to be in prayer with His Father. Jesus said, *"My people, you need to take time out for an occasional retreat. Many times i had to get away from men, so I could be in deep union with My Father and the Holy Spirit. You, also, My children, must get away from your daily tasks to renew your spiritual energy. Those who go on retreats, know what a blessing it is to be more closely united with Me."*

I could see some world leaders coming together for a conference. Jesus said, *"My people, man is proud of how many people that he can control either financially or politically. You know not how little your power is before Me. See the futility in trying to gain power over people in this world. Your fame will last but a moment and when you die, everyone will soon forget you. Seek to be with Me in Heaven and that will be enough for you to accomplish."*

I could see some towers and places to travel. Jesus said, *"My people, do not be taken up with so many desires of travel and places to be. These things may delight you for a time, but they soon pass away. Only the spiritual blessings should be sought, for they have everlasting significance. Things of this world are gone tomorrow. Things of Heaven will always please the soul and lead you to your salvation. So forget your desires for travel and become closer to Me."*

Friday, August 29, 1997:

After Communion, I again could see some hurricanes that seemed very violent. Jesus said, *"My people, these storms you can sense are near. Every day you are reading of the violence with guns in your streets. There is continued violence still being done to the unborn, but it is kept secret. There are even signs of continued preparation for nuclear war. I have told you before that your weather will turn violent as you have become a violent people. So do not be surprised that the violence in your weather reflects your society. You need to be on your knees more in prayer or your society will consume itself in chaos."*

Later, at Adoration, I could see many desks like in a classroom. At each desk, I could see a crucifix in the middle. Jesus said, *"My children, each of you are students of life and as in the vision, you need to take up your daily cross and follow Me. I did not put you on this Earth to have an easy life. This life is a testing time to see how faithful you will be to My Ten Commandments and My love. All of you are asked to suffer for My Name's sake. So do not be disappointed when you meet with grief and troubles. These things are to test your faith and see if you will seek My help or go on your own. Those seeking My help will find life less burdensome. Learn from your trials how best to trust in your Lord for everything, not just when you are in trouble. When you walk with Me constantly, you will have life much easier in following My Divine Will. Train your body in fasting and prayer and you will be able to endure any trial."*

Saturday, August 30, 1997:

At Adoration, I could see a warship cruising at sea. In the next scene, I could see thick dark smoke coming from the ship. The final scene was a ship rolling over on its side. Jesus said, *"My people, many of your nations are fighting over land or resources. Satan has succeeded in many cases in having you fight each other out of pride for your own desires. People and nations are becoming more belligerent in fighting for what they please. See, My friends, it is in your best interest to strive more for peace than physical gain. Think of the lives that are lost in such conflicts. Do not allow Satan to have his way with you. Pray for peace daily that wars may be avoided. If you do not stop your wars at the beginning, they will soon spread to involve many countries."*

Sunday, August 31, 1997:

At St. Patrick's Church, Nashua, New Hampshire, after Communion, I could see a large heart shape with concentric heart shapes telescoping inside. Jesus said, *"My people, I am trying to show you in this vision a sense of My infinite love for all of you. You are held close to My Heart and I would never abandon you. I am even pursuing you to your dying breath in order to save your souls from Satan and from being lost in Hell. I have shown you in My death for you, how much I love you. This love of mine is warm and unconditional. All I ask, is that you love Me and follow My Will for you. In the readings, it is important to follow Me in your hearts and not just in your exterior motions. You must live the Gospel message every day, so you are not a hypocrite. This means you should follow all you do by what you believe. By being true to Me and what is in your heart, no guile will be in you. It is this living in the truth and your good intentions that I look to find in each heart. Those who outwardly call Me Lord, Lord, but do not believe in their heart, will be spewed from My mouth for not truly loving Me. Come to Me in humbleness and seek My love without any of your selfish feelings in the way. I will repay all of My faithful servants with a heavenly banquet that you truly will be happy to share with Me forever."*

Later, at the Most Precious Blood Monastery, Manchester, New Hampshire, at adoration, I could see a tall angel, St. Michael, guarding this monastery. Jesus said, *"My friends, this is sacred ground where My Real Presence is being adored. I have sent My angel to be a guardian of this monastery. Those faithful here will be protected by My love for them. Remain true to your calling in your vocation and My saving power will go with you."*

Monday, September 1, 1997: (Labor Day)

After Communion, I could see a padlock and some handcuffs. Jesus said, *"My people, I am showing you how it will be when My Church will be persecuted. The churches will be locked to prevent people from worshiping God. The evil authorities at that time will try to imprison all those professing to love God, instead of the Antichrist. Some of my faithful will be captured and handcuffed. They will be led away to prisons and detention centers for My Name's sake. They will martyr, torture or enslave My remnant. You must be faithful during this testing time, even if you must endure suffering. Those who are faithful will live in the Era of Peace as their reward. So trust and have patience. Do not be afraid to go into hiding, for it may be your best protection. Be assured that I will protect your souls and lead you to safety."*

Later, at Adoration, I could see myself entering into a large cylinder of complete darkness. Jesus said, *"My people, this age is entering into a spiritual darkness where life has no value. Many millions of unborn children are condemned to death before they ever see the light of day. How long do you think I will allow this butchering to go on? At the end of World War II the killing of the Jews was stopped, but how are you to stop the killing of your infants? Why is it not possible for people to see the parallel of killing the Jews with killing the unborn? Yet, the killing goes on with only feeble attempts by some to stop this carnage. Even if you were to bribe these mothers to bring their babies to term for adoption, it would not change their hearts to holding life precious. In any way that is possible, people should be struggling to give the unborn the right to life. If this effort does not bring down abortion, then My justice will rain down a destruction befitting your sins. How many times have I called on you, America, to wake up from your own holocaust and stop killing My babies? Your time is running out before you will lose everything. The material goods that you have traded for the blood of these infants will be stripped from you. Come to Me for forgiveness even of your abortions and I will forgive you. But go and sin no more with this murderous blood on your hands."*

Tuesday, September 2, 1997:

After Communion, I saw a wicker basket that held one cob of corn and a little water in the bottom. Jesus said, *"My people, as time draws on, you will start to see the effects of poor harvests on your food supply. The poor people in the third world countries will experience this first. Then, in your turn, you will see the food growing more scarce. As a result, food prices will increase and a black market for food will increase into a contrived shortage. The rich will lord it over the poor and many riots and wars will break out over food shortages. Theft will be rampant before supplies even reach the stores. As less food will be on the stores' shelves, you will have to rely more and more on the food you have set aside. Then roving bands will seek out any food available and many will flee the cities at this time. Have faith, My children, and I will protect you. This is the situation that the Antichrist shall manipulate to his advantage. Prepare spiritually and physically, for this time will be a great test of your faith in My Words."*

Later, at Adoration, I could see a cement wall as part of a prison. Jesus said, *"My people, I have suffered much at the hands of men. I too, was a prisoner and I was tortured and whipped. I then was crucified and I gave up My life that men may have eternal life. You too, My friends, may have to suffer in prisons for My Name's sake. You may even be asked to die a martyr's death. If you are called home, you will be given a prophet's reward of eternal life with Me. So, be prepared for whatever will be asked of you. Some will be martyred and tortured during the tribulation, but I will guard your souls from evil. Evil will have its moment, but it will be of short duration. Then My justice shall call all men and spirits to judgment. It is only a small time until evil will be chained in Hell. Rejoice when this final moment will arrive."*

Wednesday, September 3, 1997: (St. Gregory the Great)

After Communion, I could see Our Lady coming in white as at Fatima. Mary said, *"My dear children, I wish to honor St. Gregory, but I am coming more for the children. As the little ones return to school, you need to help them with their spiritual lessons as well. See that they learn their prayers and give honor and worship to my Son, Jesus, on Sundays. I love all of my children, as does my Son, and I want them to know His love as it is linked to my own. Help the children as much as possible to be exposed to Jesus' love in all they do. Jesus loves the little ones so much and He does not want to see any harm befall them. So be more open in looking out for the spiritual welfare of all children. This love of God needs to be instilled in all of my little lambs. So, when you take them to school, remind them of their Spiritual Mother and their Savior, who are always watching over them."*

Thursday, September 4, 1997:

After Communion, I could see an elderly lady sitting in a pew in a church. Jesus said, *"My people, I want you to be more observant of your Christian responsibilities. For you parents, it is easy to understand how you need to care for your own children both for their physical and spiritual development. You can see how your love for your children many times moves you to help them more than just your duty. So it is with Me, when I treat you as My children and My love for you causes Me to pour out My gifts on you. I am asking you to continue in your wider family of your fellow men and women to look to help those in need. The elderly, especially, need your help in many ways. In addition to serving their physical needs, it is important to visit them and make them feel welcome and not isolated by their slower mobility. Instead of just thinking of your own life, be always ready to reach out and help your neighbor whenever an opportunity to help should arise. Remember, in all of your good deeds, that you are helping Me when you help the least in My Kingdom."*

Later, at the prayer group, I could see a sword thrust into a dark blue robe of Our Lady. Mary said, *"My dear children, I am Our Lady of Sorrows and I have had to undergo many pains in my earthly life. I am sharing with you in your earthly pains that you have to undergo. See that my trials were a blessing in disguise. You are to follow my Son and accept any trial of pain that you must undergo. Do not refuse pain, but accept it graciously, so you may give it up to Jesus. Pain is a way to humble the body and the spirit. All of you witness to some pain in your life. Use it, as I did, as a grace to become closer to your suffering Savior."*

I could see an empty chair and someone kneeling in prayer. Jesus said, *"My dear people, when you come to Me in prayer, it would help you to kneel in adoration. When you pray on your knees, you can be more disposed to Me and avoid distractions. Pray from your heart and keep focused on a statue or picture of Me. Those who come to Me with prayers of adoration or mercy for sinners have chosen the better portion."*

I could see a terrible car crash with a car tipped over. Jesus said, *"My people, when you see famous people killed suddenly, let this be a reminder to you that you are mortals waiting to die one day. This is why it is important that before you can live your life for Me, you must be ready to die and be resurrected. Life will test you dearly every day, but you know one day that you will be called to your particular judgment when you die. So prepare every day to die, for you know not when I will come for you. You must be a faithful servant, whose master will come to find following his plan. Woe to him, who is not found faithful when his life will be called from him."*

I could see a store with many flames coming out from it. Jesus said, *"My people, I have asked you to prepare for the days of tribulation when your world will be turned upside down by a brief reign of evil. You will see people burning stores to loot and there will be chaos in your streets. Do not fear these days, since My angels will protect you. Instead, be trusting in My Word that you must endure this spiritual cleansing in order to experience My Era of Peace. Be joyful that My purification will come to remove all evil from the Earth."*

I could see a large precious gemstone. Jesus said, *"My people, the Kingdom of Heaven can be like a precious gem that a man may go out and sell all that he has to buy this gem. This is how you are to be disposed to the promise of My Kingdom. The price of eternal life is worth giving up everything of this world, including your own will. You should be willing to seek My Divine Will so that nothing can come between you and Me. When you follow Me with this reservation, truly the Kingdom of Heaven will be opened to you."*

I could see a wooden clock lying horizontal on the ground. Jesus said, *"My people, I am showing you that the time of your earthly*

life is running out. That is why the clock is horizontal, represent-
ing the earthly life. Know that once you seek the vertical or spiri-
tual direction, there will be no more time. All of your earthly cares
and desires will pass very quickly. It is the spiritual direction that
you most need to be concerned about, since it will be for an eter-
nity. Seek Me in love, for I will lead you to your salvation. By
patient endurance, you will gain your crown in Heaven."

I could see some statues of some old Egyptian pharaohs. Jesus
said, *"My dear people, do not aspire for fame and riches in this*
place of torment. Look to all men over time, who had all the
earthly possessions that they needed, but they could not take it
past the grave. No matter how much man tries to make his body
immortal, he falls on abysmal failure. It is not your concern to
be well off in this world, for what will it gain you if you lose your
soul in the process? Instead, seek your treasure in Heaven and
you will be rich spiritually, which is more valuable in the next
life. You are called to live with Me in eternity, so come and enjoy
your Master's banquet."

Friday, September 5, 1997:
After Communion, I could see a black chair that was empty.
Jesus said, *"My people, I am showing you this empty chair of St.*
Peter as a sign of My Pope son's leaving Rome. The chair is black,
because an evil pope will take over his position. Be prepared at
that time, My faithful, for you will then see a schism in My Church.
This false pope will be in league with the Antichrist to try and
deceive the people not to follow Me. This false witness will bring
an abomination upon the chair of St. Peter. He will distort the
current teachings of the faith and relax all of My laws in the name
of accommodation. He and the Antichrist will be working with
Satan to try and mislead even My elect. Do not give any allegiance
to this next pope who will blaspheme Me by worshiping the Anti-
christ. When you see this evil pope deviate from the teaching of
My Revelation, you will know that it is the beginning of the end of
My schismatic Church. My true faithful will be forced into un-
derground Masses. Your current places of worship will soon be-
come corrupt in their practices. When the priests change the proper
consecration, My Real Presence will no longer be there. Pray for

spiritual strength during this coming trial of the tribulation. Pray to Me and I will provide My protection. Be at rest that you will not be long from My day of the renewed Earth. Evil must be removed from the Earth, because My justice will no longer allow its presence. Those who go down this evil path of worshiping anyone other than Me, will soon be condemned to Hell."

Later, at St. Thomas More Adoration, Denver, Colorado, I could see two parents holding each arm of a young child as they were bringing the child to church. Jesus said, *"My people, do not give up on your children at any age. Give them good spiritual direction by your example. It is your constancy in the faith and your persistence in winning their souls to Jesus that may be their salvation. Continue praying for them and gently reminding them of their duty at Sunday Mass. When you do everything possible for them, you have done your part in being responsible for their souls. The children have to make their own decisions by their own free wills. Let the children come to Me out of love, by your direction."*

Saturday, September 6, 1997:

At the Carmelite Monastery, Denver, Colorado, after Communion, I could see some Carmelite nuns dressed in brown. Then I saw Our Lady come dressed in brown with the light of the sun radiant around her. There was a vision of Marmora, Canada where Mary came to me before. Also, there was a vision of the cave at Mt. Carmel in Israel. Mary said, *"My dear little ones, it is a blessing this day that I come to share my love with you and that of my Son. You see me dressed in the light of the sun, but even more, I am dressed in the light of my Son, Jesus. I am always bringing you to Him. My dear children, the walls of this monastery are blessed as you know. You can see that those, devoted in prayer to me and my Son, are always under my protection. Those who are faithful, I hold near and dear to my heart. You must go among the people and share with them how much I love my children. As your Heavenly mother, I never let you out of my sight. I seek all of Heaven's blessings for you, to protect you with the angels from the temptations of the evil one. We cannot violate your free wills, but we ask you to follow the way of Jesus in all that you do. Come, my children, and greet your Lord wherever you can find Him in his Real Presence in the Blessed Host. Continue in your Rosaries each day for these are your spiritual weapons to fight the evil one. Continue also to wear your scapulars of my protection. Jesus and I love you so much, and we are seeking your love also in our happy family of the Body of Christ."*

Later, at St. Thomas More Adoration, Denver, Colorado, I could see a large rut on the side of a highway. Then the highway started moving back and forth until it looked like a winding road. There was a huge earthquake. In the next scene, I saw a night vision with all the lights on in the city and suddenly they all went out. Jesus said, *"My people, you must be prepared for the events about to unfold. I have given you before about an earthquake that will be coming in California. This will be severe and its timing is near. Many people there will be shaken out of their complacency. There will be much destruction and many will lose heavily in their material possessions. The second vision of the blackout is elsewhere in your country. This will be some probing by the One World people to test the power of their control. As they have a stronger position, they will be more bold in causing larger blackouts. These will be stronger signs that the Antichrist will soon come to power. Follow Me in trust and I will continue to protect My faithful."*

Sunday, September 7, 1997:

At Mother Cabrini's Chapel, Denver, Colorado, after Communion, I could see some dark fleeting shadows of demons. I then saw some white beautiful angels protecting these grounds from the demons. Mother Cabrini came and said, *"My dear pilgrims, thank you for making a visit to my shrine. By this vision, you are seeing that the protection of the angels is already present here. This is truly a refuge for sinners in many ways. I have asked all of my children to witness to my shrine. My Lord has blessed this ground and has assigned His angels to guard over this land. Be thankful for the spring of blessed water as well. When you come, I invite you to pray the Rosary on your ascent up the hill. The Lord is always reaching out to help sinners. Offer up your prayers here for all of the intentions of those souls that you are seeking help for. The Lord will hear your prayers and I will carry your inten-*

tions to Him as your intercessor. Go, my friends, and continue to bring souls close to the Lord."

Later, at St. Thomas More Adoration, Denver, Colorado, I kept seeing at least seven different bridges ruined all around the world by earthquakes. Jesus said, *"My people, I have told you in these End Times that you will see one event right after the other in quick succession. You are seeing volcanoes, earthquakes, and other storms coming together. These again are the signs of the End Times, but the people are not looking to Scripture for this interpretation. Wake up, My people, and see that your time of tribulation draws near. Even though these events will be closing in on you, have trust in My protection when this destruction meets a fever's pitch. Men will finally take notice of their losses and they will seek My help. For some, My justice for their sins will be hard to understand, but as time goes on, these events will bring sinners to their knees seeking My mercy. Know, My children, that the face of the Earth will be greatly changed during these coming days. Prepare, My children, to be tested in a way where all of your material possessions will be stripped from you."*

Monday, September 8, 1997: (Birth of Mary)

At Our Lady Queen of Peace, Denver, Colorado, after Communion, I could see Our Lady come and she was standing at the middle of a crossroads. Mary said, *"My dear children, I am happy to greet you on the day that you celebrate my birthday. You know how I was born without original sin, so I would be the proper vessel for my Son's birth. When I was born, this event set in progress the beginning of your salvation. I have been made blessed, since I had no sin. You are seeing that all roads to your salvation had to come through me by God's own design. That is why my entry into life took on more significance than any other birth to that time. By the grace of the Holy Spirit, I gave my 'yes' to Jesus and the Spirit allowed this most Sacred Conception. As you look at the succession of these events, you can see how they were all set in motion at my birth. Give praise and glory to God that He graced me with the birth of Jesus. Also, give praise to God that He sent His only Son for the redemption of all mankind."*

Tuesday, September 9, 1997:

After Communion, I could see a strange light as it traveled across the sky. Jesus said, *"My people, this light will illuminate your souls as you will flash back to all of your days. Each day of your life will be brought before each of you, to show you how I have seen all of your actions. This is an embodiment of the warning experience which all of mankind will come to know. Be prepared to evangelize the lost souls who may for a short time be predisposed to believe in Me. This God, whom some have denied, will be made real to them and they will have to make a decision to be with Me or against Me. There will be no middle ground, as everyone will be forced to choose God or not. This will be a touching moment for many souls and possibly their last change to be saved. When this event comes upon you, struggle unceasingly to bring souls back to Me."*

Later, at Adoration, I saw some gold objects. I then saw a huge crowd at a boxing match. Jesus said, *"My dear people, how is it that you are always seeking riches or watching sports? These things you have turned into earthly idols. Many treat those with money special in hopes to be returned a favor in their will. Even as someone dies, there is some fighting over the inheritance. Do not let greed for money control you, since elusive wealth is here today and gone tomorrow. Also, many are attracted to sports and even some try to make money on the outcome. Such players are paid exorbitant salaries by those willing to watch them. In a word, do not place the desire for things of this world before Me. The first Commandment says you shall have no other gods before Me. Riches and sports can become gods before Me, if you forget to give Me worship and show more interest in them. You should seek to be with Me first in your life. If anything else comes before Me, then you are an idolater of this world. Do not let Satan distract you so much with worldly things, that you forget Me. Say your daily prayers with fervor and your remembrance of Me will bring you eternal life."*

Wednesday, September 10, 1997:

After Communion, I could see two chairs opposite each other in the church. Jesus said, *"My people, there have been different factions in My Church throughout history. Even today, there are divisions between those who support my Pope son John Paul II and those who do not. These are the seeds for the future schism in My Church that will be coming. It is one thing to seek an understanding of what the teaching authority of My Church teaches. It is an entirely different thing to challenge the authority of My Church in its pronouncements of doctrine. Those who give bad example by not following My Commandments or by not following the Church's guidance in its laws are asking My judgment against them. I have given you divine revelation in the Scriptures and guidance through My Pope son's teachings. It is the responsibility of all of My faithful to be in obedience to this teaching authority of My Church."*

Thursday, September 11, 1997:

After Communion, I could see the faces of some people being arraigned for trial. Jesus said, *"My people, do not give scandal to others around you by your behavior. Many look to My faithful for example to lead good lives. If you are openly defying My laws and are carried off to jail, how can you show your neighbor good example? You must be conscious of every act that you perform in public. Some will look to criticize your every action. You must be responsible in your behavior, since it is being scrutinized by Me and your neighbor. So put on love and heartfelt mercy, so you can lead souls to Me, instead of giving bad example."*

Later, at the prayer group, I could see a cloth picture with Padre Pio's image on it. Padre Pio said, *"My friends, this picture of me is like your cloth pictures of Jesus on the shroud. He blessed me with His wounds and gave me to a prayerful life. My greatest joy was to meet Jesus in the Holy Sacrifice of the Mass. I come to you now seeking your prayers for your Pope John Paul II. He is besieged with many evil forces. He is in great need of your help at this time."*

I could see a vague golden image which was similar to the picture of St. Therese at the wedding. St. Therese said, *"My dear children, I am happy to witness this grace that I granted Amber at her wedding. Let this be a lesson to you that Heaven is listening to your every prayer. Do not be afraid to use novenas and*

fasting to petition Heaven for your needs. If it is in accordance with the Will of God, your intercessors will be allowed to grant you favors. Some favors are not as unusual as this picture, but they come to you in little ways as in a gift of roses. Reach out to others to give flowers, for they may need that little gift to raise their spirits." Note: Amber and Jarvis Garetson were married

Dec.27,1996 in Flush, Kansas. Amber prayed a novena to St. Therese for their wedding and she invited St. Therese to be present.

I could see some miracle pictures giving witness of Heaven's presence. Jesus said, *"My people, you are fortunate and blessed to receive these miracle pictures, icons, and statues. These blessings are shared with you to lift up your faith, so you are not downcast by life's trials. It is this witness to you of these miracles that should give you confidence to trust in Heaven's help. These miracles are there also to help those who are weak in faith. By these signs, many are being saved from Satan. Give thanks to God and continue to remain faithful to following Me."*

I could see a group of figures dressed in robes and they all were glowing with a golden light like angels. Mark came and said with permission: *"My son, these are your guardian angels who are constantly at your side. They are in darkness because of your evil age and all of its corruption. But they give their light to show you your way each day. Pray to your guardian angels, since you will be needing their help during the tribulation. By seeking their help, you will see what a grace from God that their help can be. Even in your darkest hour, a prayer to them will lead you out of despair."*

I could see a large steering wheel and many clouds of unknown in the future. Jesus said, *"My people, many times you are upset and uncertain of what the future will be. Do not be so concerned with the unknown tomorrow, when you have enough trouble dealing with the known of today. Each day brings its own problems, but if you ask My help, I will walk you through each experience. Trust in My help and you will have nothing to fear."*

I could see Mary holding the baby Jesus. Mary said, *"My dear children, every time a new baby is born, there is joy over a new soul to share your life with. There was much joy at my birth and more so for my Son's birth. Look at each newborn infant as an image of my Son and treat each life as precious, since the Holy Spirit is present in each life. Do not even contemplate for a moment the taking of any life at any stage of its development. As you reach out in love to each infant, you will see why my Son holds them in a special part of His heart. You need to teach this to everyone, especially those considering an abortion."*

I could see a subway with lights coming from the windows. Jesus said, *"My people, by your Baptism I have placed you on a path to Heaven. Those who give their will over to Me find this path to their liking. Those who get off this path to follow their own will, many times find more trouble than the greener pastures they are seeking. Be content with your lot and never seek to be someone that you are not. In life your curiosity may be your undoing. So stay close to Me in a humble life, not seeking to be famous, but only a soul searching to be with Me in Heaven. When you find the right path again, you will wonder why you decided to leave Me in the first place."*

Friday, September 12, 1997:

At Holy Family Adoration, Ogden, Utah, I could see an outline of Mary. Then I saw Jesus on the Cross superimposed over Mary. Mary said, *"My dear children, come to your mother, who longs to hold you in her arms. I place my mantle of protection over all of my children. How blessed you are to have the gift of faith in our Two Hearts. When you come to me, I am always leading you to my Son, Jesus. In His Real Presence of the Blessed Sacrament, give your heart and soul over to my Son's Will. Listen to the direction He wishes to give to each of your souls. You will see that walking with my Son will make your life so beautiful and full of hope. Do not let the worries of life drag you down, but lift up your hearts so Jesus can make you one with His Heart. His love is gracious and He wishes to share His blessings with all of you. Seek Him in all you do and you will be filled with a heavenly joy that no one can take from you. Follow my Son in all of the sacraments that He lays before you. Drink in a good measure of His kindness and your salvation will be provided for you. Never doubt in His love and protection and life in my Son will be given you. See that being in my Son's Presence is all that your soul is craving."*

Later, at Holy Family Church, Ogden, Utah, after Communion, I could see several crosses over some tombs in a cemetery. Jesus said, *"My people, I call on you to remember that one day you will all be called before Me in judgment. Be prepared, My little ones, to meet Me where all of My faithful will be given their reward. You should not think so much of this world's goods, but be concerned most with your heavenly destination. Every soul has been redeemed with My Blood and you are called to be with Me by your own free will. Seek My forgiveness in Confession so that your soul will be always ready to receive Me. My children, you must live each day as if it were your last, for you know not when I will call you home to Me. By doing everything for Me each day, you will always be in readiness to receive Me. Pray and guard your souls from the evil one, for your souls are your most precious possession beyond anything else."*

Saturday, September 13, 1997: (Triumph of the Cross)

At the Abbey of Our Lady of the Holy Trinity, Huntsville, Utah, after Communion, I could see some beautiful mountains in complete daylight. (We came in the dark.) Jesus said, *"My people, I am showing you how beautiful this country is in giving witness to My glory. My children, these places of prayer and dedication to My Will are places of Holy Ground. Those who give worship to Me and have given over their worldly opportunities will receive My protection at all times. These places of refuge truly will be sources of grace against the evil one. Your angels will show you to such places during the tribulation for your own protection. Have faith and trust in Me that you will be guided to these safe havens. All of these things, that I have shown you, are a grace to know and understand My love and My mercy. For those who are faithful to Me in their prayers and their good works, I will be guarding over your souls."*

Later, at Our Lady of the Mountain Church, Jackson Hole, Wyoming, after Communion, I could see Mary come dressed with a crown. Mary said, *"My dear children, I wish to share with you in the triumph of our Two Hearts over the evil one. It was through my instrumentation and God's design that my Son came into the world to die for man's sins. I was at my Son's death at the foot of His Cross to witness His death for all mankind. By His suffering on the Cross, Satan and sin were defeated. Before He died, He asked me to be the mother of all men through St. John, the Apostle. Jesus has appointed me to crush the head of Satan as his defeat will be completed. Be joyful and have faith and hope in my Son's promises to resurrect you to Heaven. It is by His Blood that you are now free. He has redeemed all souls by the triumph of His Cross. Just as Satan thinks that he has won the battle, my Son will crush him. Both at his death and the conquering of the Anti-christ, evil will always be subjected to His divine power. Give praise to God for His glorious Resurrection and His future chaining of the evil one in Hell."*

Sunday, September 14, 1997:

At Our Lady of the Mountain Church, Jackson Hole, Wyoming, before the Blessed Sacrament, I could see an entrance to a well-decorated church with flowers and a prominent Holy Water fountain. Jesus said, *"My people, when you come into church, you need to bless yourself properly with the Holy Water. Do not just make it a trite gesture. Holy Water, properly blessed, has the grace to keep the demons away from you. When you bless yourself with the sign of the Cross, you are affirming your faith in the Blessed Trinity. Again, with this sign you are giving witness to the redemption of man's sins by My death on the Cross. All of this takes place when you bless yourself with the Holy Water. So, make it your intention to make this sign reverently and concentrate on the true meaning of what you are doing."*

Monday, September 15, 1997: (Our Lady of Sorrows)

After Communion, I could see a circle of nuns dressed in black looking down towards me. Mary said, *"My dear children, my life was a life of sorrow from the moment of Simeon's prophecy to me. I was always living in the shadow of knowing one day that such great trouble would befall me. All of these trials I had to suffer along with my Son. I had to witness the cruelty of my own people chastising my Son for trying to save their souls. It was the height of sorrow for a mother to hold her own Son's dead body off the Cross. Even today, I am still sorrowing over those souls who are still rejecting my Son. Remember, my children, how much my Son loves you, that He died to save all mankind. Remember that it was your sins that hurt Him so much. He must cleanse all the sins of mankind in order that each of you may be open to coming to Him in salvation. He has paved the way for each of you to Heaven with His suffering. You must suffer also, in carrying your own cross in this life. Pick up your cross lovingly and accept my Son's rule over your life. By walking with Him and me to Calvary, you too, will have your resurrection into the glory of His heavenly banquet."*

Later, at Adoration, I could see some heavy construction vehicles making roads and detention centers. Jesus said, *"My people, I am showing you how the One World people are working feverishly at their plan of internment. Many new roads and new places of detention are being built now. Their plans for takeover, using the mark of the beast and enforcement by the UN troops, are moving ahead rapidly. This construction has to be in place for them to move people from their homes to better places of control. I am asking you, My people, to prepare your sacramentals and a few necessities for hiding. The events I have told you about previously are soon to be implemented. You will have to leave soon when these things begin to happen, or you will be captured and tortured in these death camps. The Antichrist and Satan's forces will soon be moving to declare themselves in control. Pray, My children, and follow My angels as I have instructed you. I will protect My faithful from being brainwashed to worship the Antichrist."*

Tuesday, September 16, 1997:

After Communion, I could see a picture of red with an anchor. Jesus said, *"My people, you are being tested especially by the evil of your day. That is why you are seeing the red color of the demons from Hell. Yet, you have an anchor of hope and trust in Me, who has all power over the demons and evil men. No matter how strong these evil men claim to be, I will humble them and bring them to their knees. Have faith in My Word and follow My commands and you will enjoy a life eternal. I will protect My faithful from all the cunning of the evil one's plans. His reign will be brought down just as he arrives on his throne. This I will do in the sight of all mankind to bring down all the proud and arrogant who have no respect for their Creator. I tell you, those, who appear to rule now, will soon be chained in Hell."*

Later, at Adoration, I could see an arm with some strange marks on it. Jesus said, *"My people, beware of the coming diseases and pestilence that will be coming in the last days. You will see new vaccine resistant strains of germs that will again cause huge epidemics of sickness. Even some diseases will be brought about through germ warfare. Your manipulating of the genes in medicines and plants will be another cause for concern. Those gifted with healing these diseases will be sought out. See, those who defy My love will have to suffer many plagues here as their punishment at the end of this age. As many will die from these outbreaks, there will be much chaos and terror for those who survive. Be faithful to Me in adoration and in your prayers, and I will protect you from these new germs. See that all these things will happen to confuse the proud and bring low those seeking fame."*

Wednesday, September 17, 1997:

After Communion, I could see Jesus lying on the Cross and it was flat on the ground in the dark. Jesus said, *"My people, you must be willing to suffer with Me each day and endure the hardships that befall you. When you reach out to Me for help, I will be walking with you as you carry your cross. Still, there are some who completely forget about My help. These are the same ones who do not want to hear about suffering. They want to be pampered and live a comfortable life without worries. They also want to depend only on their own resources. You may have enjoyment for a while, but soon everyone will have to endure trials. This life is fragile and only a testing place. For those living only for themselves, they will have a much harder time when things go bad, and they do not have My help to fall back on. So, live your life following My Will and look to Heaven for your enjoyment. This life is only temporary, and you will never find complete rest here. You can only gain Heaven if you pick up your cross and bear it lovingly for Me. Give Me your burdens, and I will lighten your load."*

Thursday, September 18, 1997:

After Communion, I could see a man upright in a tomb. Jesus said, *"My people, this day I am calling on you to die to self. This means that you are to give up your love of self for My sake. By taking up your cross and living in Me and for Me, you will be*

1979р. МАТИ ТЕРЕСА

rejecting the world's ways in order to follow My Will. I have cre-
ated all of you to know, love and serve Me. You have been given a
free will by which you can come to love Me, by choice and not by
force. I am an all-loving God of all of My creatures, and I call on

you to love Me in return for all I have done for you. You have been given life, and My faithful have been blessed with a gift of faith as well. You are in the world, but you are not to be of the world. So, do not let the pleasures and desires of the body lead you away from Me. Seek My grace to love God and your neighbor without your own selfishness interfering with My love. The more you love Me and others, the closer you will be to your salvation."

Later, at the prayer group, I could see a cross pictured as an icon with Jesus on it. Jesus said, *"My people, you see Me suffering on the Cross because My Church has been divided between east and west and even among many religions. All of My souls on Earth make up one people of humanity which needs to worship Me to be saved. You need to be more united in your battle against the evil one. The more you join together in prayer, the stronger you will be at the tribulation when you will need your spiritual strength."*

I could see some large statues being destroyed. Jesus said, *"My people, many statues and crucifixes are being removed willingly from the churches and the hospitals. When you remove these heavenly reminders of the saints, you are not seeking their help in fighting the evil of this age. Your bare churches are a testimony of the weakening of your faith. You have pictures of your relatives at home. Why should you not keep remembrances of the saints and angels in your church? Pray to all intercessors in Heaven to help you in this evil age. They are very willing to help you keep on the narrow road to Heaven."*

I could see a leaf falling and darkness followed. Jesus said, *"My people, when you see the leaves start to fall, you know that winter and long nights are coming. Even now as you see the signs of the End Times coming, you know the darkness of the brief reign of the Antichrist will soon be upon you. But, rejoice My people. As I came as the Light of the World in the middle of the longest nights at Christmas, so I will come as a great light in victory to renew the Earth at the end of the tribulation."*

I could see a man and a horse, and there was a golden glow as the sun shone all around them. Jesus said, *"My people, you are all created in My Image and after your Baptism, you glowed with a beauty in your soul. Do not lose that initial fervor for Me when you were first converted. Do not become stagnant in your faith, but move to enrich it by frequenting the sacraments and follow-ing My Will. When you continue on your faith walk to Heaven, never stop desiring to be with Me forever. I am the goal of your soul to know and love."*

I could see some Coptic lanterns as near Jesus' cross on Calvary. Jesus said, *"My people, it is good to reverence My holy places, especially where you have My Real Presence in the Blessed Sacrament. It is good to have the statues and traditional adoration places for remembering Me, but it is even more important to have your presence before Me. By your public adoration of Me, you are witnessing your faith before men. When you spend time often in adoration, many will see how much you love Me and it will be genuine and not just for show."*

I could see some poor people and then Mary showed me her lovely face to witness to them. Mary said, *"My dear children, look at the poor all around you that are reaching out for help. Take a lesson from Mother Teresa in how she led her sisters to help everyone in their dying moments. All souls are equal before the Lord and you need to give honor even to the poor. You have seen how one woman's acts of kindness inspired others to imitate her in bringing poor souls to my Son at death. Think to do acts of mercy for all those who cross your path. Do not turn aside pleas for help, but do what you can for those in need. Remember my Son and the Holy Spirit are with every soul."*

I could see parts of a map of the United States and it was all in khaki green. Jesus said, *"My people, what you are seeing is an armed camp that will be dominating your country. You will see armies suddenly take over your country, and they will imprison many in detention centers. Religious persecution will be rampant, and you will need to seek My refuges for safety. Pray, My children, to keep your sacramentals with you to fight this demonic attack. See this is a religious battle of good vs. evil. It is this last battle that all of you will be heading to. Seek My help and that of your angels, and you will find consolation in My protection."*

Friday, September 19, 1997:

After Communion, I could see a row of houses and a huge flood of water was going down the road in front of the houses.

Jesus said, *"My people, more floods are to come, but they are a part of the cleansing process that must continue in your hearts. As the readings warn of the influence of money, you do not need to be rich to be happy. Happiness should come in being able to help others, especially in bringing them to Me. When you cleanse your earthly desires for riches, you will see that living modestly is much better for the spirit. For others who want to cling to their luxuries and comforts, many of these will be stripped from you. So, seek Me first in My Kingdom, and all of your needs will be cared for. Do not seek to be rich in the world, but seek Me to be rich in the spirit and you will have chosen the better portion."*

Later, at Adoration, I could see a satellite of one of the space probes. It was all dark around it as something was about to happen to it. Jesus said, *"My people, My mother has requested your prayers for peace because of the possibility of a nuclear war. I am adding to that possibility a nuclear fallout from both satellites and an incident at a nuclear plant. This kind of incident can be mitigated with enough prayer. Unless men and women take this request seriously, you could see a nuclear incident. Pray to hold back My justice of such an incident. Many of these problems you have called down on yourselves. For the sake of the just people, I will allow your prayers to intercede in this case. Pray much that this suffering will not strike the Earth. If it should happen, there will be much suffering and death in many*

To LOVE Means to SHARE

parts of the world. This is another sign of the End Times in refer-
ence to Wormwood in the Bible which contaminated the waters."

Saturday, September 20, 1997:

After Communion, I could see a stone wall and then a for-
tress castle. Jesus said, *"My people, I want you to be more loving*
toward your neighbor in all of your dealings. When you are
mistreated, continue to show your love for them. Do not build
walls of mistrust or hate between your fellow men. In a word,
you are to be perfect in loving your enemies as your friends. For
all of you are made to My Image and all are worthy of your love.
When you show your love, do not have any grudges and do not
talk of others in gossip. When others see your love, they will be
moved by your holiness and may be converted. Others are al-
ways watching your actions to see if you live by what you preach.
So, do not be hypocrites and live in the truth, and you will have
nothing to fear. When you have love for everyone and Me, you
will have peace in your heart. Continue to pray and give good
example of your love for Me by showing love and concern to
help all of your neighbors."

Later, at Adoration, I could see Jesus up close as He was suffering on the Cross. Jesus said, *"My people, pride is to be rooted out of*
your life, if you are ever going to follow My Will. Many feel good
about themselves when they have been successful in the eyes of
the world. Some even measure their success in how much wealth
that they have amassed. My friends, do not let worldly traditions
and worldly goals direct your lives. You have seen when I came
and preached the truth, the men of My day let their pride prevent
them from believing. It was too hard for some to give up all their
earthly things to follow Me. Even more so, they did not want to
suffer in any way. They killed Me because they only wanted to
follow their own plan and not God's plan. Today, man is no differ-
ent, since he has to deny himself to follow My Will. Many again
have too many comforts and too much pride to admit following My
ways are the best for their souls. If you have trouble giving over
the reins of your life to Me, then you may be like the Pharisees and
do not want your life changed. Yet, unless you give up your com-
forts and suffer for My sake, how can you purge the body of all its

lusts for the things of this world? You may be knowledgeable in some things, but you must become like little children if you are to enter into Heaven. Practice being humble, and rely only on My help to lead you through life. Being a fool for Me in the eyes of the world takes courage in the abuse you may undergo. Those spiritual things of value and the virtues that you need to reach Heaven take time and work to develop. Enter the narrow gate in full submission to the Divine Will, and you will win the greatest prize that your soul could desire—eternal life with Me in Heaven."

Sunday, September 21, 1997:

After Communion, I could see some glowing green demonic eyes. I then saw some images of wolves with an evilness about them. Jesus said, *"My people, you need to be aware that the devil is a real being. He is Lucifer, the fallen angel. He tempts you daily to sin and you must be aware that he wants to destroy all souls on Earth. You must be conscious that people are sinning, even though they do not want either to know it or be told about it. Sinners do not want to be told of their sins, since they will no longer be able to have their bodily pleasures. For those that want sin to be revealed to them, let me show you things some do not even think are sins. Having intercourse before marriage; using contraception even when you are married; masturbation and any other unnatural means to prevent conception such as vasectomies and tying of the tubes in women. Other sins concern ruining other's reputations with gossip, slandering others, cheating employees out of their just wages and benefits. Whenever you violate My Ten Commandments as in doing harm to your neighbor or not worshiping Me on Sundays, you need to be sorrowful for your sins and seek My Forgiveness of them. I know you are weak and sin, but I have enabled you to return to grace through My Sacrament of Reconciliation before the priest. It is important to seek out a good confessor who will direct you to properly live by My Will and not by your own ideas. Those who relax My laws for a better hearing will have to answer before Me at the judgment seat. I come in love to bring you to a stronger love for Me, but you must be willing to prune the evil out of your heart. Come to Me before it is too late and you lose yourself in Hell."*

Later, at Adoration, I could see a farm tractor and it was being suspended by a large strap from over head. Jesus said, *"My people, your farmers are being financially pressured by bad crops and high costs. Many smaller farmers will be forced out of business. This will lead to a food crisis and possible shortages. Prices will be more controlled because of only a few in control. Food will soon be used as a means to control the people. I have told you to prepare for a famine by storing up extra food and water. The ability to buy and sell food will get increasingly difficult until supplies will be limited. This is when you will need your own supplies. Much chaos will ensue as people become desperate for food. This may bring about the need to go into hiding sooner as stealing and killing for food will be rampant. This is the condition that I have told you will make it ripe for the Antichrist to take control—during a general crisis. This also will be a time of financial unrest all over the world. Prepare, My people, for your trials are about to begin."*

Monday, September 22, 1997:

After Communion, I could see some very tall mountains on opposite sides. Down the middle there was a great plain that had several large heart shapes. Jesus said, *"My people, this vision is showing you the site of an awesome battle that will take place as the Antichrist seeks full reign of the world. The hearts on the battlefield indicate how My help and My angels will assist the good forces in defeating evil. Have trust, My people, that I will come to your aid and your protection will be assured. This final battle of good and evil at Armageddon will decide once and for all the almighty power that God has over all creatures. It is God's Will that will be done, and the demons and evil men will be chained in Hell. Then there will be no dispute over who reigns over the world, for My triumph will rise over the heaped bodies of My enemies. My glory will shine forth over the Earth, as it will once again be made over into the Kingdom that it was meant to be."*

Later, I could see a foreign land and there were people holding hands in fellowship with each other. Jesus said, *"My people, no matter where you go in this world, there will always be some people who will show you love and a willingness to help you. It is good that you keep close to those faithful in your prayer groups. You need to reach out to all men to help them, even though many will reject your belief in Me. I am uniting all of My faithful throughout the world, because soon you will be tested by the tribulation. By your common prayer, you will be able to help each other in enduring your evil age. Come and join Me wherever you see two or more gathered in My Name. I will be in your midst leading you to safety. Trust in Me, My children, and this short trial will be over. Follow My Will throughout your life, and you will find the true path to your salvation."*

Tuesday, September 23, 1997:

After Communion, I could see some people trying to avoid seeing others. Jesus said, *"My people, many times you are unwilling to accept advice from others. Sometimes your pride is so overwhelming, that you fail to advance because you do not want to use the ideas of others. Over time, you become shame-faced as you realize that others can have better ways of doing things. This is the same lesson in you spiritual help. You cannot overpower the devil on your own. There you are dealing with angels who have more power that you can ever have by yourself. Instead, you must rely on My help to get you through life. I will not force My help on you. You must seek it out on your own. As in life, see that My ways are better than your ways in leading you to spiritual perfection. I am here always willing to help you. See the light and humble yourself by letting your will conform to My Divine Will. By accepting that My plan is better for you, you will be able to advance spiritually as well."*

Later, at Adoration, I could see some figures fighting with swords over some gold treasure. Jesus said, *"My people, since the time of Cain, man has been killing each other over riches, land or fame. Some want to get rich so quickly that they will steal to get their wish. My people, do not seek other men's possessions, for they will not bring you any joy or fulfillment. Seek only heavenly riches which will help you reach your goal—to know the Lord more fully. The more you give up your earthly riches to follow Me, the more you will be rewarded in the next world. So do not place your trust in earthly riches, for they will fade away*

*by thieves or rust. Where will all of your built-up wealth go when
the tribulation comes? Others will take what you have, so do not
fear losing it. When I come in triumph, be the watchful servant
ready to receive your master."*

Wednesday, September 24, 1997:

After Communion, I could see a waterspout as an aerator on a
reservoir. Jesus said, *"My people, look at this vision as the waters
of My endless graces. I am showing you the abundant graces
that are available to those that seek them. The cleansing waters
of Baptism were the first you received in washing away original
sin. For those who come to Me in the Sacrament of Reconciliation, again there are the cleansing graces to remove all of your
mortal and venial sins. Still there are many prayers, novenas,
and fasting that you can do to relieve even the temporal punishment due for your sins. All of these graces are present for you.
All that you have to do is make that forward effort to come to Me
and request them. Many sinners wallow in their sins and the discomfort of the despair of not being refreshed by My help. Assist
these poor souls in any way to bring them to Me to be forgiven.
They still must exercise their free will to be saved. Just help them
with your spiritual prodding to put them back on course to their
salvation. Many souls are headed for Hell unless they pull out of
their laziness to repent. Without that urging to be cleansed of
their sins, they may be buried in the world's ways, never to see
My light again."*

Thursday, September 25, 1997:

After Communion, I could see a footstool and it was suspended
in the clouds. Jesus said, *"My people, you are My heavenly foot-
stools; My servants whom the Master will find working for Me
when I come to call all men to Me. Just as My priests are My
representatives on Earth, you, My faithful, are My arms and legs
on Earth as well. You are the ones that I depend on to reach out
in faith to witness My Word to all who will listen. Many sinners
are downcast and in despair among the trials of life. But in you
they may find the light of faith, the strength of My graces that I
offer to each soul through My Sacraments. See how much I de-*

pend on you to bring Me to others. As My ambassadors then, you must set a good example to others of how I want everyone to live. I need your leadership in this battle of good and evil. You cannot stand idly by in this fight, but you must jump into action and fight the good fight. Carry My torch of faith, so that others, who see you, will want to come to Me. Remember you must remain prayerful and fasting, for your center of strength lies in Me. Join others around you in prayer and go forth to teach all nations of My salvation for their souls."

Later, at the prayer group, I could see some angels as they lifted their trumpets to announce the triumph of Jesus. Jesus said, *"My people, take notice that all of Heaven is in anticipation of My intervention in the affairs of men. This evil age has called out for My judgment. I have been long in coming, giving you many hours in which to repent and be saved. Many have abused My time of mercy to continue in their sins. I will be coming to judge the people of this age. You will know by My warning how I see all of your sins. As the feast days of the angels will soon be upon you, look to their help during the time of the tribulation."*

I could see the baby Jesus in a manger. Jesus said, *"My people, many have talked of 'El Niño' and of how it will affect your weather. Know that this refers to the time of My Birth and its name is of Me as an infant. It is fitting that the judgments of your chastisement will be associated with My Name. These storms to come are the ones I have told you that would test you. These storms again will be more signs of the End Times, since they will be more difficult than others seen in your age."*

I could see Jesus in a large light from Heaven, and He was looking down on the poor souls in Purgatory. Jesus said, *"My people, these poor souls are encouraged by the preparation being made in Heaven. They sense the great battle on Earth which is beginning. They know at the end of the coming Era of Peace that they will be drawn up to Heaven. Pray for these souls that their burden of suffering may be lessened. Do not forget to pray for your own relatives in this place of torment, for many have fallen lax in their prayers."*

I could see some people walking amidst the flames on Earth. Jesus said, *"My people, these are the living dead who will suffer the flames and plagues of the last days. This punishment will be directed to all those evil souls who have rejected Me despite all of My pleas to save them. I ask you to read in the last book of the Bible how such men and women will be tortured. I beg all of My souls to come to Me now before you will suffer this fate. Much like My chosen ones who will have Heaven on Earth, so the evil people will experience Hell on Earth. I set this choice before you, to choose life or choose death."*

I could see those in their evil deeds with a bright light being shown on them. Jesus said, *"My people, do not think that the evil deeds that you do in secret will go unnoticed. I tell you soon a time of illumination will come upon you. You will see all of your evil deeds exposed before all of Heaven like in broad daylight, only brighter. Your sins of crimson red will be shown you. This warning time is, for some, your last opportunity to realize how evil you have been. Heed this chance and seek forgiveness of your sins. Although your sins be scarlet, I will receive you into conversion. Free yourselves of all of your sinful ways, and come walk in the light of My Truth."*

I could see a large vigil light burning while there was fire and chaos in the cities. Jesus said, *"My people, come join in a vigil of prayer for all those souls who need your help to be converted. I will protect My faithful during the tribulation, but these souls must come to Me now. Your prayers will be powerful even more so in this age, but many will fall victim to Satan's forces of evil. Show all who will listen that I am their only means to salvation."*

I could see Mary appearing to many throughout the world. She was holding out her mantle of protection to all of her children. Mary said, *"My dear children, thank you for all of your Rosaries to-night for all of my intentions and yours. Continue your prayers, for they are your best weapon against evil. I have witnessed to many of my dear ones to give witness of my Son's coming tri-umph. There will come a time soon when I will no longer be al-lowed to appear to you. Look to this as another sign of the End Times. My Son is appearing to many now and these also will cease. As the day of the Antichrist comes, hold your Rosaries and scapu-lars high and evil will have no power over you. Teach others to use these sacramentals as their weapons against the demons."*

Friday, September 26, 1997:

After Communion, I could see a woman with a frown on her face. Jesus said, *"My dear children, you must be radiant with joy and share in My jubilation that man is about to be freed of his remaining bonds of slavery to sin. Lift up your spirits and cheer up your drooping frowns, for you have every reason to be happy at this time. At My Death on the Cross your shackles of sin were released. The promise of My Kingdom is upon you. Even in this evil age you still have access to My grace in the sacraments. In a short time, man will be freed from his remaining effects of original sin. You should be rejoicing at the thought of the new Era of Peace that will be coming in the near future. All that you are required to do is to bear your cross patiently with faith in Me and soon all of your troubles will be gone. I have fulfilled My promise of salvation, and soon My promise of this age of peace will be upon you. So be thankful that you are living in this glorious time of My grace and mercy. It is true that you may have to suffer for a while, but after this brief trial, you will be sharing in the paradise*

that Adam once enjoyed. When the devil will be chained in Hell, you will have an opportunity for gaining in spiritual perfection that you have never dreamed of. My love will so envelop the Earth that you will understand the feeling of the Heaven on Earth."

Later, at Adoration, I could see an old Mass going on at the altar facing away from the people. Jesus said, *"My faithful people, you, who were brought up years ago, remember My statues and the old altars. It was not necessarily the physical things in the church, but the faith that was instilled into you by your parents and the nun teachers. This experience of a proper understanding of the faith is now missing in the teaching of the children. Many schools are teaching feelings and social justice rather than how to love Me and obey My commandments. My believers, you must share your faith experience with those around you. If the faith you know and love in Me is not passed on, how can anyone have faith when I return? You are seeing the abominations and the apostasy that I told you would come in the end days. You must struggle as My remnant remaining true to My Word, no matter how others will criticize you. It is the truth of My Words that many cannot tolerate, because it would force them to follow My Will and not their own. Pray, My children, for your suffering will not be much longer. Even though I am allowing many atrocities to exist, I will soon come to judge the Earth and cleanse it of the evil which has gone beyond its bounds. Understand that My justice is being called down on the Earth. This is not a message of doom and gloom, but a message of hope that evil will be taken away. You have all reason to be joyful in anticipation of My triumph over Satan. This evil will be allowed a time to test all men. With My help, it will be My faithful that will endure, for your love for Me is carrying you on even against difficult odds."*

Saturday, September 27, 1997:

After Communion, I could see the Host being raised at an underground Mass. Jesus said, *"My people, in your day you are accustomed to having Mass in your churches every day. Soon you will be fortunate to find a faithful Mass in an underground church. I will be with you in a miraculous way even during the tribulation. See how fortunate you are to receive Me in Com-*

munion. It will become even more of a treasure to you when the Mass will be restricted. Your churches will be closed and a schism will fall all over the world. There will be great turmoil among My faithful, but you must have trust in My protection. Pray for your Spiritual Communion and your angels will deliver My Host to your lips. Rejoice, My people, for I will never leave you helpless."

Later, at Adoration, I could see trees in a woods with the sunlight shining on green leaves. Jesus said, *"My people, why do you concern yourself with money when it will not mean anything in the tribulation. You are so taken up with your comforts and planning to have enough money. Your money will buy you nothing, since you will need the mark of the beast to buy and sell. When you go into hiding, you will depend solely on My help for your survival. So do not fight or quarrel over the money that will mean nothing. Both your time here and your wealth are fleeting things. Your spiritual wealth is more worth fighting for, since it is this measure that will help you into Heaven. So, when you help your neighbor and give to charity, you are storing up wealth that no one can take from you."*

Sunday, September 28, 1997:

After Communion, I could see a grotto with some water flowing. Jesus said, *"My dear son, I am affirming the gift of prophecy I am working in you through the Holy Spirit. You have listened to My call and you have been willing to go forth and preach a message of repentance when it is not popular. You have been given beautiful words of love and faith which I have asked you to share with everyone. At the same time, I have given you messages of preparation that many have found uncomfortable. This is not unusual in the prophets that I have sent in the past. Many of My prophets were killed and mistreated because of the message of My judgment. So it is with your day; I have given messages of warning that the people do not want to hear. You must accept criticism and continue the mission that I have given you to strive to save souls. Do not be afraid to speak out in My Name to help the people know that I will be at their side even during the fear of the tribulation. I have blessed you in many ways with the struggle in this mission. The warning messages still need to be told to wake up the people in their sin. Keep focused on Me in prayer and help souls to the sacraments and pray over them when they come to you. This is an important task that I ask all of My prophets to continue preaching, even when some will persecute you. Speak My truth, so your responsibility to tell them is carried out. It is up to these souls to discern and take action in coming to Me in conversion."*

Later, at the reunion Mass, after Communion, I could see a dark cloud and a dark oil poured out from it. Jesus said, *"My people, I am showing you how to see that the evil man pours out evil from the storehouse of evil in his malicious heart. The good man pours forth love and obedience to God from his storehouse of good in his heart. That is why I look to the heart for the intentions of that which you are doing. It is by the fruits of your labor that you can tell if a man is good or evil. So it is with My prophets; you can test if they are true or not by the fruits of their actions. Those who do everything in My Name are close to the Kingdom of God. All of you are called to be prophets, for I have asked you all to preach My Word to all the nations. This is the glory of each of your lives that you lead as many souls as possible to Me and convert their lives of sin."*

Monday, September 29, 1997: (Archangels' Feast)

After Communion, I could see a large clock and it turned into a complicated antenna. Jesus said, *"My people, man has prided himself on his many scientific accomplishments. Still, you are limited by your sinful nature from original sin. Even more so, your being and your powers as a human are very small compared to the universe and the angels. When man thinks that he is so powerful, he should consider the powers around him. My angels and I far surpass any of your powers. See yourself as one of My creations in a large universe and do not be puffed up with any pride. Instead, follow the example of the good angels, who are constantly giving Me praise and glory. Be thankful for the guidance and protection which My angels provide for you."*

Later, at Adoration, I could see a staff with a cross on it being held up. Jesus said, *"My dear son, do not fear your persecutors. Continue on in the mission I have given you, without any doubt or fear. You have asked the purpose of this mission and how to answer those who are critical. I am telling you to always obey My Magisterium. It is My Pope who is most vocal on sin and repentance. The bishops and priests of your day, for the most part, are not speaking out about sin, conversion, and a return to Confession. Look at the messages coming forth from the visionaries that I send before you. My mother and I are constantly encouraging prayer and preparation for My coming again. Many clergy are afraid to speak out on the evils of your day as abortion and sins of the flesh, since they fear the loss of donations from people who would be upset. My messengers need to seek souls to be converted from their sinful lives. I am also calling My messengers at this time, as I called Jonah, to preach of the impending judgment. I have told you that the only sign I will give you is that of Jonah. Jonah preached of My wrath to come and the people repented in sackcloth and ashes. I am calling you as Jonah to preach the same message—unless the people repent, My judgment and chastisement will fall on them. This is not doom and gloom or a message of fear, it is a wake-up call to all of those steeped in sin. Unless these souls are awakened, they could be lost forever. As in the Gospel, he who preaches in My Name, has My Word in his heart. Who has the right to stop My messengers from saving souls? It is true to discern, but your time to save souls is short. Listen to My words and act on them. Do not be fearful of your critics. As long as you are sincere in following My Will to save souls, how can you be in error? Trust in My Words before you trust in the words of men."*

Tuesday, September 30, 1997:

After Communion, I could see a black leaf connected to a branch. Jesus said, *"My people, I am the vine and you are the branches. You cannot live apart from Me. I give you sustenance in your soul with My heavenly food of bread and wine. I provide for you in the physical world with all the seed-bearing plants and the animals for meat. It is good to believe in Me, for all I have revealed to you in the Scriptures. These are the gifts that I have bestowed on you and it is important to make them a part of your life. See around you as the leaves begin to fall, that they are dead once they are separated from the vine. Those separated from Me spiritually are dead as the black leaf. At the same time, the seasons represent to you the circle of life and death in the physical world. It is thus in the fall that you should have thoughts of how you will prepare for your death. You know that everyone has to answer to Me on the judgment day. Your preparation in life is to always be ready in your heart for the day I come, by keeping your souls in grace away from sin. Be ever faithful to Me in your daily actions, and you will have nothing to fear. I love you all so much, and I long for the day to bring all of My faithful to Heaven."*

Later, at Adoration, I could see crosses with the corpus on it, standing as pillars among a crowd attending a football game. Jesus said, *"My people, even if I were to witness My Presence at such an event as a football game, the people would still be mesmerized by their desire to watch the game. Man, today, is tested by many attentions for his time. Now more than ever, there are many distractions from following My Will. Those who share their time with Me are truly dedicated faithful, since Satan has many ways to hold your interests. I ask you to make a special effort to keep focused on Me, since your time to be here grows shorter with everyday's passing. When you reach out to Me for My love and peace, time is suspended for a while. When you take time to give Me adoration, you are giving Me your precious time to thank Me for all that you have. In the quiet of your heart, I love to come and give you My rest. Life can be a burden for you, but when you let Me have the reins of leading you, it becomes a joy. Share with Me in your prayers and your needs and I will bless you with My many graces."*

Index

abortion
  holocaust like the Jews (Jesus)   9/1/97
  sins of the flesh (Jesus)   8/28/97
  violence kept secret (Jesus)   8/29/97
Adam
  share in paradise (Jesus)   9/26/97
Adoration
  gives us rest (Jesus)   9/30/97
  witness of faith (Jesus)   9/18/97
angels
  blowing the trumpets (Jesus)   9/25/97
  call on them for help (St. Michael)   7/20/97
  call on them in need (Mary)   7/5/97
  chain demons, evil people (Jesus)   7/15/97
  lead to refuges,share love (Jesus)   7/24/97
  protection from Antichrist (Jesus)   9/15/97
  sound trumpets last days (Jesus)   8/9/97
Antichrist
  agents of the UN (Jesus)   7/26/97
  chip to buy and sell (Jesus)   8/24/97
  control mind (Jesus)   7/24/97
  control of UN troops (Jesus)   8/8/97
  control through devices (Jesus)   7/29/97
  declaration not far off (Jesus)   8/7/97
  general crisis,financial (Jesus)   9/21/97
  manna, angels, refuge (Jesus)   7/9/97
  see as father of lies (Jesus)   7/24/97
  to declare himself (Jesus)   9/15/97
antipope
  in league with Antichrist (Jesus)   7/4/97
apostasy
  stay true to God's Word (Jesus)   9/26/97
apparition site
  golden glow of love (Mary)   7/31/97
apparitions
  soon ending (Mary)   9/25/97
Archangels
  power & gratitude (Jesus)   9/29/97
Armageddon
  victory over evil (Jesus)   9/22/97

armaments
  will not save us (Jesus)   7/17/97
Assumption
  give our 'yes' (Mary)   8/15/97
astrology
  do not follow (Jesus)   8/26/97
Australia
  Rosaries for protection (Mary)   7/17/97
Baptism
  soul glows (Jesus)   9/18/97
Battle of Armageddon
  pray for peace (Jesus)   8/7/97
  separate good and evil (Jesus)   8/14/97
battle of good & evil
  Antichrist, bankers, One
    World (Jesus)   7/16/97
  seek God's & angels' help (Jesus)   9/18/97
behavior
  give good example (Jesus)   9/11/97
bicycles
  gas shortages, tracking (Jesus)   8/4/97
blackout
  One World people testing (Jesus)   9/6/97
Blessed Mother
  birth free of sin (Mary)   9/8/97
Blessed Sacrament
  encourage Exposition (Jesus)   7/30/97
  give respect (Jesus)   8/18/97
  reverence, gift of love (Jesus)   7/11/97
  reverence,thanksgiving (Jesus)   7/4/97
blessings
  give thanks,honor,glory (Jesus)   7/3/97
bodily appearance
  keep natural beauty (Mary)   8/7/97
Carmelite Monastery
  place of protection (Mary)   9/6/97
caves
  precedence in Bible (Jesus)   7/10/97
  protection in persecution (Jesus)   8/25/97
children

day care and abuses (Jesus) 8/7/97
do not give up on them (Jesus) 9/5/97
parents' responsibility (Jesus) 8/7/97
parents', grandparents' help (Jesus) 7/17/97
spiritual education (Mary) 9/3/97
take to Mass, trust (Jesus) 7/14/97
teach faith (Jesus) 8/11/97
China
influenced by evil (Jesus) 7/8/97
choices
determine Heaven or Hell (Jesus) 7/25/97
choose life
or choose death (Jesus) 9/25/97
Christian responsibility
to children and elderly (Jesus) 9/4/97
Church
divided, East & West (Jesus) 9/18/97
will survive split (Jesus) 7/2/97
churches
burned, go underground (Jesus) 7/24/97
closed & persecuted (Jesus) 9/1/97
circle of life
found in seasons (Jesus) 9/30/97
comet
cataclysm of conversion (Jesus) 8/21/97
on track for Earth (Jesus) 8/10/97
commandments
seek forgiveness (Jesus) 9/21/97
consecrate homes
protection, Belgium (Jesus) 7/10/97
Consecration
August 15, preparation (Mary) 7/5/97
evangelize, Two Hearts (Mary) 7/13/97
contraception
vasectomies (Jesus) 9/21/97
conversion
speak the truth (Jesus) 9/28/97
corporations
employers abuse workers (Jesus) 7/24/97
creation
seek a higher authority (Jesus) 7/6/97

crucifixes
test the spirits (Jesus) 8/21/97
death
do not worry about pain (Jesus) 7/22/97
destruction
humbled by powers (Jesus) 7/3/97
detention centers
National parks, U.N. (Jesus) 7/10/97
some faithful captured (Jesus) 9/1/97
UN, One World people (Jesus) 9/15/97
discipleship
practice what you preach (Jesus) 8/7/97
diseases & epidemics
germ warfare (Jesus) 9/16/97
Divine Will
give our will over to (Mary) 8/26/97
Kingdom of Heaven open (Jesus) 9/4/97
divorce
separations (Jesus) 8/27/97
doom & gloom
a real message of hope (Jesus) 9/26/97
wake-up call (Jesus) 9/29/97
dress properly
causes sin (Jesus) 7/31/97
earthquake
in California near (Jesus) 9/6/97
earthquakes, volcanoes
signs of the End Times (Jesus) 9/7/97
will reshape the land (Jesus) 8/21/97
Egypt
use of evil for good (Jesus) 7/11/97
El Niño
storm chastisements (Jesus) 9/25/97
employees
just wages & benefits (Jesus) 9/21/97
entertainment
distractions of the world (Jesus) 8/7/97
Era of Peace
after purification (Jesus) 9/4/97
after purification (Jesus) 8/8/97
coming soon (Jesus) 9/26/97
trust and patience (Jesus) 9/1/97

Eternal Father
  prayer group dedicated
    (God the Father)   8/14/97
eternity in Hell
  feeling of how long (Jesus)   7/21/97
Eucharistic miracles
  Real Presence (Jesus)   8/13/97
evangelization
  give witness (Jesus)   8/16/97
evangelize
  conversion time is short (Jesus)   8/24/97
  Heaven rejoices (Jesus)   8/23/97
  messages, wakeup call (Jesus)   7/17/97
  most important task (Jesus)   7/27/97
  must act quickly (Jesus)   7/20/97
  save souls (Jesus)   8/18/97
  serving lost souls (Jesus)   7/25/97
  suffering, persecution (Jesus)   7/1/97
  with double speed (Mary)   7/13/97
evil
  allowed for a test (Jesus)   7/15/97
  do not give credit to evil (Jesus)   7/15/97
Exodus experience
  led by angels (Jesus)   7/31/97
eyes of faith
  puts life in perspective (Jesus)   7/28/97
faith
  fight the good fight (Jesus)   9/25/97
  in old Church (Jesus)   9/26/97
fame and riches
  store spiritual treasures (Jesus)   9/4/97
family
  under evil attack (Jesus)   7/27/97
famine
  prepare food and water (Jesus)   7/9/97
farmers
  food shortages (Jesus)   9/21/97
Fatima Statue
  close of visit in Rochester (Mary)   8/22/97
Final Judgment
  end of Era of Peace (Jesus)   8/2/97

flakes
  found on the floor (Mary)   7/10/97
floods & fires
  chastisements for sin (Jesus)   8/1/97
floods and storms
  chastisement of America (Jesus)   8/28/97
food crisis
  Antichrist control (Jesus)   8/8/97
food shortages
  food multiplied (Jesus)   8/11/97
  riots, contrived (Jesus)   9/2/97
  weather, One World (Jesus)   7/3/97
football
  mesmerized by desires (Jesus)   9/30/97
free will
  die to self (Jesus)   9/18/97
freedoms
  spiritual and physical (Jesus)   7/3/97
friendship
  love over hate (Jesus)   8/14/97
gene manipulation
  cause for concern (Jesus)   9/16/97
gold icon
  Statue of Fatima, help (Mary)   8/2/97
gossip
  live in the truth (Jesus)   9/20/97
graces
  Baptism & Confession (Jesus)   9/24/97
Great Chastisement
  prepare yourselves (Jesus)   8/14/97
grieving
  give consolation (Jesus)   8/14/97
guardian angels
  show you the way (Mark)   9/11/97
hearts opened
  spiritual spring cleaning (Jesus)   8/5/97
helicopters
  mapping targets (Jesus)   7/26/97
Hell
  path full of good intentions (Jesus) 7/25/97
  repent of laziness (Jesus)   9/24/97

Hell
    understanding eternity (Jesus)   7/21/97
    best protection (Jesus)   9/1/97
holy ground
    Abbey of Our Lady, Trinity (Jesus) 9/13/97
    Mt. Sinai,holy spots (Jesus)   7/7/97
Holy Spirit
    help in presentations (Holy Spirit) 7/10/97
Holy water
    power, take into hiding (Jesus)   7/22/97
    sign of the cross (Jesus)   9/14/97
home schooling
    a special grace (Jesus)   8/7/97
homes
    food & religious articles (Jesus)   8/7/97
hope and trust
    evil will be destroyed (Jesus)   9/16/97
hospitality
    forgot God & neighbor (Jesus)   7/29/97
humility
    conform to Divine Will (Jesus)   9/23/97
    path to Heaven (Jesus)   9/11/97
icon
    turned to gold at home (Mary)   7/31/97
Immaculate Conception
    mission as Mother of God (Mary)   7/5/97
infants
    preciousness of life (Mary)   9/11/97
intentions
    God looks into hearts (Jesus)   9/28/97
Jesus' Presence
    Real Presence in Host (Jesus)   7/12/97
Jonah
    messengers preach as (Jesus)   9/29/97
Joseph famine
    will repeat today (Jesus)   7/9/97
joy
    slavery to sin ended (Jesus)   9/26/97
judging
    owner of the vineyard (Jesus)   8/20/97

judgment
    Confession,be prepared (Jesus)   9/12/97
    spiritual preparation (Jesus)   8/21/97
justice
    evil removed from Earth (Jesus)   9/5/97
King of the Universe
    honor & respect (Jesus)   7/6/97
last days
    punishment & plagues (Jesus)   9/25/97
leaders
    called to high moral order (Jesus)   7/15/97
life on Earth
    time running out (Jesus)   9/4/97
living bread
    strength to reach Heaven (Jesus)   7/8/97
love
    mortar of society (Jesus)   8/25/97
Magisterium
    always obey (Jesus)   9/29/97
manna
    brought by angels (Jesus)   8/8/97
    in tribulation (Jesus)   8/17/97
    spiritual & physical food (Jesus)   7/18/97
mark of the beast
    to buy and sell (Jesus)   8/8/97
Marmora
    Our Lady of Mt. Carmel (Mary)   9/6/97
marriage
    as God loves the Church (Jesus)   8/27/97
    Covenant relationships (Mary)   7/19/97
    unity in family (Jesus)   7/3/97
Mars
    man as spec in space (Jesus)   7/6/97
martyrdom
    some called to (Jesus)   9/2/97
Mass
    goes underground (Jesus)   9/27/97
    union of Jesus with us (Jesus)   8/18/97
Masses
    churches closed (Jesus)   8/14/97

materialism
  strip your idols (Jesus)   7/17/97
messengers
  no right to stop (Jesus)   9/29/97
miracle icons,satutues
  lift up faith (Jesus)   9/11/97
miracle picture
  prayer answered,wedding
    (St. Therese)   9/11/97
Monastery
  protected by an angel (Jesus)   8/31/97
money
  choice of God vs. money (Jesus)   7/10/97
  seek Heaven (Jesus)   9/19/97
  will mean nothing (Jesus)   9/27/97
money and riches
  trust in God (Jesus)   7/31/97
monied men
  Sodom & Gomorrah (Jesus)   7/1/97
mortality
  always be ready to die (Jesus)   9/4/97
Mother Cabrini Shrine
  protected by angels
    (Mother Cabrini)   9/7/97
Mother Teresa
  help poor souls (Mary)   9/18/97
Muriel
  family message (Muriel)   8/15/97
Name of Jesus
  overwhelming power (St. Michael)   7/20/97
National Shrine
  Immaculate Conception (Mary)   7/5/97
New Jerusalem
  Era of Peace (Jesus)   8/2/97
Noah
  rainbow covenant (Jesus)   8/14/97
novenas & fasting
  temporal punishments (Jesus)   9/24/97
nuclear accident
  nuclear plants (Jesus)   9/19/97

nuclear war
  pray consecration (Jesus)   8/14/97
  sign of preparation (Jesus)   8/29/97
One World people
  refuse to go to war (Jesus)   7/27/97
  stripping defenses of US (Jesus)   7/17/97
Our Father
  always present (God the Father)   8/14/97
Our Lady of Sorrows
  salvation (Mary)   9/15/97
Padre Pio
  pray for Pope,shroud cloth
    (Padre Pio)   9/11/97
peace
  pray for, stop fighting (Jesus)   8/30/97
perfection
  love your enemies (Jesus)   9/20/97
permanent sign
  refuges of protection (Jesus)   8/19/97
Perpetual Adoration
  blessing on parish (Jesus)   8/28/97
persecution
  continue in mission (Jesus)   9/29/97
  do not want to hear Word (Jesus)   9/28/97
  seek God's protection (Jesus)   8/1/97
Pilgrim Statue of Fatima
  thanks to workers (Mary)   8/28/97
place
  pray for leaders (Jesus)   8/28/97
Pope John Paul II
  speaks out on sin (Jesus)   9/29/97
  will flee when he's exiled (Jesus)   8/4/97
power
  seek Heaven, not control (Jesus)   8/28/97
prayer
  avoid distractions (Jesus)   9/4/97
  sign of love (Jesus)   8/28/97
prayer groups
  help each other,tribulation (Jesus)   9/22/97
  source of strength (Jesus)   8/25/97

pride
   accept advice (Jesus)   9/23/97
   follow God's Will (Jesus)   9/20/97
   give thanks for gifts (Jesus)   8/16/97
   man small in universe (Jesus)   9/29/97
priests
   representatives on Earth (Jesus)   9/25/97
   uphold the Gospel,faith (Jesus)   7/7/97
Princess Diana
   remember we are mortals (Jesus)   9/4/97
priorities in life
   evangelize (Mary)   8/2/97
prophecy
   affirm personal gift (Jesus)   9/28/97
prophets
   test the fruits (Jesus)   9/28/97
Purgatory
   pray for poor souls in (Jesus)   9/25/97
purification
   Scripture fulfilled (Jesus)   8/19/97
pyramid
   One World symbol of evil (Jesus)   7/11/97
Queenship
   hearts are one (Mary)   8/22/97
reconciliation
   cleansing of sins (Jesus)   7/28/97
   seek good confession (Jesus)   9/21/97
   wipers for rain (Jesus)   8/5/97
refuge
   manna as in Exodus (Jesus)   8/21/97
refuges
   prepare for the tribulation (Jesus)   7/24/97
   underground Masses (Jesus)   8/3/97
religious persecution
   angels will protect you (Jesus)   7/17/97
remnant
   joy to His heart (Jesus)   7/20/97
   preserve Church,articles (Jesus)   7/4/97
   share in triumph (Jesus)   8/8/97
resurrection
   our redemption (Jesus)   7/22/97

retreats
   renew spiritual energy (Jesus)   8/28/97
riches of world
   do not bring happiness (Jesus)   9/23/97
Rosaries
   spiritual weapons (Mary)   9/6/97
   touched with blessings (Mary)   7/10/97
Rosaries & scapulars
   power over Antichrist (Mary)   9/25/97
   protect children (Jesus)   7/17/97
Rosary
   pray for Mary's intention (Mary)   7/24/97
sacramental
   fight evil (Jesus)   9/18/97
sacramentals
   take into hiding (Jesus)   8/21/97
sacraments
   prepare for hiding (Jesus)   9/15/97
Sacrifice of the Mass
   daily bread (Jesus)   8/17/97
safe haven
   interim refuge (Jesus)   8/21/97
safe havens
   rural areas (Mary)   8/4/97
Saints
   imitate lives,thanks (St. Therese)   7/10/97
Santa Fe Cathedral
   Franciscan missionaries (Jesus)   8/16/97
Satan
   lurking for souls (Jesus)   8/22/97
satellite
   nuclear accident,prayer (Jesus)   9/19/97
satellites
   monitor your calls (Jesus)   7/24/97
scapulars
   for protection (Mary)   9/6/97
schism
   authority in Church (Jesus)   9/10/97
   evil pope, bad teaching (Jesus)   9/5/97
   faithful underground (Jesus)   8/25/97
   trust in protection, angels (Jesus)   9/27/97

self-control
  bodily habits, excesses (Jesus)   8/7/97
signs
  miraculous water (Mary)   8/26/97
  no dates, Confession (Jesus)   7/31/97
signs of the times
  renew the Earth (Jesus)   9/18/97
sin
  spiritual laziness (Jesus)   8/23/97
sins
  a slap in the face to Jesus (Jesus) 7/12/97
  Jesus still suffers (Jesus)   7/19/97
sins of the flesh
  forgiven in Confession (Jesus)   7/4/97
  know what they are (Jesus)   9/21/97
  reckoned at the judgment (Jesus)   7/31/97
souls
  have a price (St. Anne)   7/26/97
sports
  earthly idols (Jesus)   9/9/97
St. Michael
  more powerful than Satan
    (St. Michael)   7/20/97
St. Peter as rock
  Pope is authority (Jesus)   8/19/97
stairway to Heaven
  carry daily crosses (Jesus)   7/3/97
statues & crucifixes
  removed from churches (Jesus)   9/18/97
statues & icons
  weeping (Jesus)   8/7/97
statues and pictures
  on walls of church, home (Jesus)   7/4/97
storms and hurricanes
  reflect violence in society (Jesus) 8/29/97
substance abuse
  pray for problems (Jesus)   7/31/97
suffering
  carry cross daily (Jesus)   8/9/97
  daily crosses (Jesus)   9/17/97
  means of salvation (Jesus)   8/14/97
  spiritual glasses (Jesus)   8/23/97

talents
  witness of glory to God (Jesus)   7/27/97
technology
  knowledge just surface (Jesus)   7/10/97
  Satan's organization (Jesus)   8/12/97
temptations
  keep prayerful life (St. Michael)   7/20/97
Ten Commandments
  test of faith (Jesus)   8/29/97
traditions
  from the heart (Jesus)   8/18/97
Transfiguration
  presence of Trinity (Jesus)   8/6/97
Transubstantiation
  Sacrifice of the Mass (Jesus)   8/3/97
travel
  final trip to Heaven (Jesus)   8/10/97
  passing delights (Jesus)   8/28/97
  seek spiritual goals (Jesus)   8/12/97
trials
  trust in God, fasting (Jesus)   8/29/97
trials and tests
  prepare with prayer (Jesus)   7/17/97
tribulation
  face of Earth changed (Jesus)   9/7/97
Trinity
  Baptism in Jordan (Jesus)   7/23/97
triumph
  justice on Earth (Jesus)   9/26/97
  of good over evil (Jesus)   7/21/97
  of Two Hearts (Mary)   8/21/97
  Two Hearts (Mary)   9/13/97
trust
  in daily trials (Jesus)   9/11/97
TV & computers
  two-way communication (Jesus)   7/29/97
Two Hearts
  seek God's Presence (Mary)   9/12/97
U.S.A.
  time is running out (Jesus)   9/1/97
UN troops
  in our country (Jesus)   7/17/97

unconditional love
    follow the Divine Will (Jesus)   8/31/97
underground Masses
    for faithful (Jesus)   9/5/97
United Nations
    detention centers,US park (Jesus)   7/10/97
    troops abused, Antichrist (Jesus)   8/8/97
United States
    armed camps (Jesus)   9/18/97
    will fall from within (Jesus)   7/17/97
Vigil of Prayer
    for conversion (Jesus)   9/25/97
vine and branches
    need for life (Jesus)   9/30/97
visionaries
    call to conversion (Jesus)   9/29/97
visitors
    show peace and love (Mary)   7/3/97
war
    over oil or money (Jesus)   7/27/97
    senseless killing (Jesus)   7/31/97
warning
    a sign given (Jesus)   7/2/97
    evangelize lost souls (Jesus)   9/9/97
    sins exposed to light (Jesus)   9/25/97
wars
    gain in intensity (Jesus)   8/21/97
    greed and power (Jesus)   7/3/97
weapons
    spiritual, not guns (Jesus)   7/24/97
white luminous crosses
    protected by angels (Jesus)   7/7/97
world depression
    economic collapse (Jesus)   8/24/97

More Messages from God through John Leary

If you would like to take advantage of more precious words from Jesus and Mary and apply them to your lives, read the first three volumes of messages and visions given to us through John's special gift. Each book contains a full year of daily messages and visions. As Jesus and Mary said in volume IV:

> *...there will come a time when you will be banned from speaking and you will rely on your books to spread the message.* Jesus 6/26/96

> *Listen to my words of warning, and you will be ready to share in the beauty of the Second Coming.* Jesus 7/4/96

> *I will work miracles of conversion on those who read these books with an open mind.* Jesus 9/5/96

Prepare for the Great Tribulation and the Era of Peace
Volume I - *Messages received from July 1993 to June 1994*
ISBN# 1-882972-69-4 . . . . 256pp. - $7.95

Volume II - *Messages received from July 1994 to June 1995*
ISBN# 1-882972-72-4 . . . . 352pp. - $8.95

Volume III - *Messages received from July 1995 to July 10, 1996*
ISBN# 1-882972-77-5 . . . . 384pp. - $8.95

Volume IV - *Messages received from July 11, 1996 to Sept. 30, 1996*
ISBN# 1-882972-91-0 . . . . 104pp. - $2.95

Volume V - *Messages received from Oct. 1, 1996 to Dec. 31, 1996*
ISBN# 1-882972-97-X . . . . 120pp. - $2.95

Volume VI - *Messages received from Jan. 1, 1997 to Mar. 31, 1997*
ISBN# 1-57918-002-7 . . . . 112pp. - $2.95

Volume VII - *Messages received from April 1, 1997 to June 30, 1997*
ISBN# 1-57918-010-8 . . . . 112pp. - $2.95

Other Great Titles From
QUEENSHIP PUBLISHING
From your local Catholic bookstore or direct from the Publisher

Trial, Tribulation and Triumph
Before, During and After Antichrist
Desmond Birch
ISBN# 1-882972-73-2 .... $19.50

The Amazing Secret of the Souls in Purgatory
An Interview with Maria Simma
Sr. Emmanuel of Medjugorje
ISBN# 1-57918-004-3 .... $4.95

After the Darkness
A Catholic Novel on the Coming of the Antichrist
and the End of the World
Rev. Joseph M. Esper
ISBN# 1-57918-048-5 .... $14.95

Mary's Three Gifts to Her Beloved Priests
A Deeper Understanding of Our Lady's Messages to Fr. Gobbi
Rev. Albert Shamon
ISBN# 1-57918-005-1 .... $2.95

The Final Warning
And a Defence Against Modernism
Paul A. Mihalik, Sr., Lt. Colonel USAF (Ret.)
ISBN# 1-57918-043-4 .... $4.95

A Light Shone in the Darkness
The Story of the Stigmatist and Mystic
Therese Neumann of Konnersreuth
Doreen Mary Rossman
ISBN# 1-57918-044-2 .... $12.95

A Little Catechism on the Holy Rosary
Miguel Guadalupe
ISBN# 1-882972-78-3 .... $4.95

Call of the Ages
The Apparitions and Revelations of the Virgin Mary
Foretell the Coming of Evil and an Era of Peace
Thomas W. Petrisko
ISBN# 1-882972-59-7 .... $11.95